ORDERS
OF
ARCHITECTURE

R. A. CORDINGLEY

DOVER PUBLICATIONS, INC.
MINEOLA, NEW YORK

INDEX

Bibliographical Note

This Dover edition, first published in 2015, is an unabridged republication of *Normand's Parallel of the Orders of Architecture*, originally published by Quadrangle Books, Inc., Chicago, in 1951, and reprinted from the first English edition of the work, originally published by A. Pugin, London, in 1829.

Library of Congress Cataloging-in-Publication Data

Normand, Charles Pierre Joseph, 1765–1840.
  [Nouveau parallel des ordres d'architecture des Grecs, des Romains et des auteurs modernes. English]
  Orders of architecture / R. A. Cordingley.
    pages cm
  "This Dover edition, first published in 2015, is an unabridged republication of Normand's Parallel of the Orders of Architecture, originally published by Quadrangle Books, Inc., Chicago, in 1951, and reprinted from the first English edition of the work, originally published by A. Pugin, London, in 1829."
    ISBN-13: 978-0-486-79574-4
    ISBN-10: 0-486-79574-8
  1. Architecture—Orders. I. Cordingley, R. A. (Reginald Annandale), 1896–1962, editor. II. Title.
NA2812.N7 2015
721'.36—dc23   2014036055

Manufactured in the United States by LSC Communications
79574803   2020
www.doverpublications.com

INTRODUCTION

NORMAND'S *Parallel of the Orders of Architecture* is unusual in this class of publication in that it includes not only a fully representative selection of those standardised versions of the respective orders evolved by certain celebrated " modern " masters of Italian or French Renaissance architecture, but also a fine series of measured drawings derived from the actual monuments of Greek or Roman antiquity still surviving. As the " Orders " composed by the Renaissance writers were based on these very structures, we are consequently afforded a means of critical comparison as well as a wide opportunity for discrimination in the selection of proportions and details appealing to our individual taste. But we may only do justice to this excellent collection of drawings by an appreciation of the circumstances which attended the growth of the orders and a realisation of their underlying significance.

THE GREEK ORDERS

The story of the Orders begins in classical Greece. There, about the eighth century B.C., we find a " post and lintol " architecture, already artistically refined beyond essential structural needs, in process of translation from wood to stone. Though none of the ancient timber work has survived, almost every stone feature is recognisably derived from a wooden counterpart. It is an architecture of colonnades, in which regularly spaced columns support a deep horizontal " entablature ", made up of a variety of members arranged in three main parts, known respectively as the " architrave ", the " frieze ", and, at the top, the " cornice " (Plate A). The columns have decorative capitals, and these serve as the principal means of distinguishing one order from another.

At the outset there were only two orders, the " Doric " and the " Ionic "; differing versions of the one architecture as produced by the two main branches of the Greek race. Most of the Dorians were settled in the Greek mainland or in Southern Italy and Sicily and the majority of the Ionians along the coasts of Asia-Minor. For the rest, their settlements intermingled. The Dorians practised a simple, direct style, of which the outstanding attribute is its virility (Plate 7). The milder, luxury-loving, Ionians produced a daintier, more decorative and varied style, indicative of their acquaintance and contacts with the near-Eastern civilizations (Plate 26).

Early Greek buildings mostly were temples, and colonnades of the Doric or Ionic orders served to give dignity to them (Plate 70). The temples were simple box-like structures, about twice as long as wide.

At the core was the " naos ", a windowless chamber shielding the sacred image. A great door, or pair of doors, when open for the religious ceremonies at the altar outside, allowed the naos a dim diffused light. The colonnades surrounded the naos completely, at a distance sufficient to provide an ample passage-way behind, themselves supporting the margins of a gently-sloping tiled roof, which made shallow gables, known as " pediments ", over the short ends of the building. The pediments comprised enframing horizontal and sloping cornices, and within each the central space, or " typanum ", was decorated with sculpture.

The only other architectural element it is necessary here to mention is the " anta " (pl., antae), a reflection of the design of a column onto the end of a short spur wall, the plan of the anta consequently becoming rectangular rather than circular. The longer sides of the walls of the naos of the normal temple projected a little to form an inner porch, and it is at the end of such walls that the antae are invariably found (see plan of Parthenon, Plate 70). The anta capital is a series of mouldings in the case of the Doric order (Plates 5 and 6), as also in instances of the Ionic order in Athens (Plate 20), though the profiles are by no means exact replicas of those of the corresponding column capitals. The anta capital of Ionic Asia Minor is even less like the design of the attendant column capitals, having a face appearance not unlike that ancient musical instrument, the lyre.

Thus the colonnades were almost the whole sum of the architecture of the early Greeks, and the initial two orders were decorative alternatives in which it might be expressed. Yet each of the two orders, Doric and Ionic, had sprung from a structural system and, although their parts ultimately became decorative, had their origin in members essential to support or protection. After the translation from timber, Greek architecture merits the description of " a carpentry in marble ". At first, the stone Doric order was extremely ponderous and squat in its proportions, but as knowledge of the capacities of stone developed, the order became progressively lighter and nearer to the proportions which it presumably had possessed before the conversion from timber. Apart from this consistent trend, the stone Doric order changed little in character from first to last. The columns of the temple of Poseidon (Neptune) at Paestum, built about 450 B.C. (Plate 8), are only four and a half times their own diameter in height, whilst those of the Parthenon (432 B.C., Plate 5) measure 5.48 times their own diameter.

In the case of the Ionic style the process of elongation of the proportions is by no means so marked, for the probable reason that, at first, only the columns were converted into stone, the entablature continuing for a while to be made in wood. Thus no extra burden of weight was thrown onto the columns and they could remain slender, like their timber forerunners. Again, whilst the Doric entablature regularly had the three main parts, architrave, frieze and cornice, the Ionic tradition in Asia Minor appears to have required only two, architrave and cornice. By the middle of the sixth century B.C. at the latest, the two-part entablature also had passed from timber to stone, as fragments from the "Archaic" temple of Artemis (Diana) at Ephesus (c. 560 B.C.)—one of a sequence of temples upon the same site—survive to show. In Asia Minor the tradition of the two-part entablature was remarkably persistent and the type probably was universal there for the chief temples until the third century B.C. It chances that none of the Plates in the body of this book illustrate the original two-part form of the Ionic entablature. Plate 26 shows the temple of Minerva (Athena) Polias at Priene (c. 335 B.C.) as having a frieze, but this is now adjuged incorrect. The true original arrangement of the entablature is shown in Figure 2 a.

Though at all times slender, the tendency towards further elongation of the proportions of the stone Ionic order is sufficiently great to be remarked. The columns of the temple on the Ilissus (c. 448 B.C., Plate 20) are 8.25 diameters in height, whilst those of the North Porch of the Erechtheum (c. 421 B.C., Plate 22) are 9.50.

Entablatures of the two orders diminish appropriately in depth as the attendant columns become lighter. In early Doric temples the massive entablature is frequently half the height of the supporting columns, whilst later, as in the Parthenon, it is reduced to less than one-third. The entablature of the Ionic temple on the Ilissus is approximately one-quarter of the column height—considerably lighter, it will be noted, than the contemporary Doric—whilst at the Erechtheum the proportion has decreased to about one-fifth.

Despite the lightening of proportions, the Greek Doric order of classical times never became so slender as to require a base to the columns. The column shaft tapered upwards quite appreciably and in most examples there was at the same time a slight outward swelling of the profile, reaching a maximum at about one-third up the height, intended to counteract an optical illusion of hollowness which parallel or near-parallel lines seem readily to occasion. This corrective subtlety is known as "entasis". The shafts always are ornamented with vertical shallow "flutes", concave channellings which meet one another on a sharp edge or "arris". Twenty is the usual number. The column capital has only two simple main parts, an "abacus", square on plan, supported by a rounded "echinus". In early examples the profile of the echinus is bulbous and widespreading; in later temples it makes a very subtle convex curve, thrusting outwards at about 45° from the line of the column.

The distinguishing features of the Doric entablature are the deep, plain architrave, the large "triglyph" blocks in the frieze, and a continuous series of shallow, wide "mutules" in the cornice, which from the fact of their sloping in sympathy with the incline of the roof, appear to represent the stone translation of wooden rafters. The triglyphs in their turn probably were

originally great wooden beams, spanning the temple from side to side. They are decorated on the face with vee-shaped vertical grooves, reflecting the upward trend of the flutes of the columns. There are twice as many mutules as triglyphs, and usually, twice as many triglyphs as columns. The spaces between the triglyphs are known as "metopes" and frequently served as a field for low-relief sculpture.

The finest Greek instances of the orders are found in Athens and vicinity. Athens at first practised the Doric style almost exclusively, like the majority of the cities of the Greek mainland, but because of distant racial affinities and her political importance, was receptive of influences from Ionic Asia Minor. In fifth century B.C. Athens, there were as many fine instances of the Ionic as of Doric. This joint practice of the two styles had important consequences.

Because of its slenderness, the Ionic column invariably has a moulded base. The original Asia Minor form of the base is shown in (a) and (b) of Figure 1. The whole base is circular on plan. The lower of the two main elements is drum-shaped, though the sides are slightly concave: the upper takes the form of a large roundel known as a "torus" moulding. Both elements are elaborately enriched with flutes or with "beads" (small roundels). The Athenian examples (d) and (e) in the diagram, both dating from the fifth century B.C., illustrate the introduction of a new main element, a second torus moulding, which soon became larger than the first. Between them, the concave element shrank in importance but deepened into the characteristic profile of a "scotia" moulding. As a whole the profile shown in (e) of the figure constituted the famous "Attic" base, used thereafter until modern times with little modification except that a square (on plan) plinth, initiated too in Asia Minor, comes to be added at the foot as a still further normal adjunct. Profile (c) in this Figure 1, illustrates the conservatism of Asia Minor Ionic, for it still shows the original arrangement of members although it is approximately a century later in date than the much more highly developed Athenian examples (d) and (e).

The Ionic shaft has less strongly marked entasis than the Doric. It is fluted, but the flutes are deeper and the normal is 24, against the 20 of the Doric. Instead of meeting on a sharp arris they are separated by a small plain band or "fillet". The column capitals are distinguished by elaborate scrolls or "volutes", which sweep like a partly-opened inverted scroll of parchment across the top of an echinus, circular on plan like the similar feature of the Doric capital. Above the volute band is a very shallow abacus, with a moulded edge. Originally the abacus was rectangular, the greater dimension running in the line of the entablature, and the volute scrolls projected widely beyond the line of column. In the Athenian instances (e.g., the Erechtheum, Plates 22-24) the abacus has become square on plan and the volutes are drawn more closely together. The Erechtheum capitals are exceptionally rich and decorative, and have a band of ornament below them which is not usually

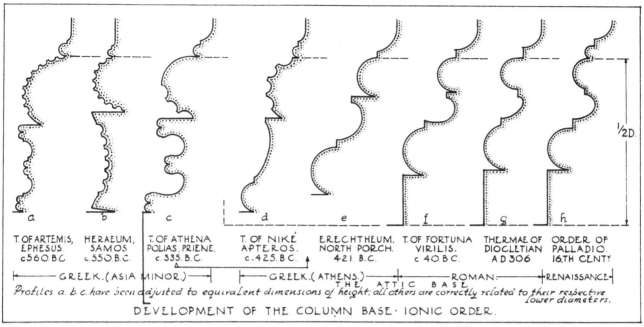

GREEK.(ASIA MINOR.) ——— GREEK.(ATHENS.) ——— ROMAN ——— RENAISSANCE

THE ATTIC BASE

Profiles a. b. c. have been adjusted to equivalent dimensions of height; all others are correctly related to their respective lower diameters.

DEVELOPMENT OF THE COLUMN BASE · IONIC ORDER.

Figure 1. Development of the base of the Ionic order.

present. The front and back faces of the normal Ionic capital are identical in design ; on the sides, the volute "cushion" is seen, elaborated in typical Asia Minor fashion with numerous flutes and beads, separated by fillets. This two-faced arrangement produced difficulties at the angles of a building which had to be met by the use of a·special diagonally-canted volute (Plates 23, 26).

The typical form of the Ionic architrave suggests that the arrangement in timber which it reproduces was that of a series of two or of three flat wooden plates, placed one on top of the other, each represented in the stone form by a fascia (Figure 2). Among the group of mouldings constituting the original form of the cornice, the chief is that of the "dentil" band, the dentils, as the term suggests, being large tooth-like projections, which seem definitely to represent former rafter or beam ends. The dentil band and the principal moulded members immediately above and below it together constitute the "bed-moulding", occurring beneath another important element, the "corona", a deep plain band which projects strongly beyond the face of the building. Figure 2 shows how persistent this bed-mould was to be.

The adoption of the Ionic order in Athens and the Greek mainland brought it under the influence of the Doric, and an immediate result there was the addition to the entablature of a frieze (Figure 2, c). Unlike the Doric, the Ionic frieze was continuous and architecturally plain, though often decorated with low-relief sculpture. Temporarily, the bed-mould was ejected and Athenian fifth-century cornices show little below the projecting corona band except a simple small moulding. The bed-mould returned into use again in due course, as has been shown earlier, though the frieze remained henceforward

a regular part of the entablature.

Instances such as the last show that as time progresses there is some tendency for the orders to lose their initial purity, and interact upon each other. For the most part, however, they retain their original characteristics through Greek times, despite the practice, which became notable in the fifth century B.C., of using the two orders in the one building. Often there were structural advantages in doing so. The Greeks did not come to understand the principle of the triangulation of wooden roof-members until possibly the third century B.C. and so had to provide frequent pillar supports inside their buildings. In the Doric order, a clumsy device was used internally sometimes, of standing one tier of columns upon another, to give support to the roof beams. If a single tier of columns of the normal Doric proportions had been used in such positions, the columns would have been massive indeed, and the useful interior space much diminished. On the other hand, the Ionic columns, with their greatly enhanced slenderness, could reach superior heights with much less sacrifice of useful room. In the world-famous Parthenon at Athens there were two inner apartments (Plate 70). The larger had a double range of super-imposed Doric columns ; the smaller, much more nearly square, four Ionic columns spanning the total height to the beams. Another fifth-century instance of the conjoint use of the two orders is the Propylaea, the entrance portal building (432 B.C.) to the Acropolis, the sacred enclosure at Athens within which the Parthenon stood. The approach way rose at an incline through the Propylaea, so that the Doric colonnades of the front and the rear porches were at different levels. They were connected by two lines of Ionic columns, placed at right angles to

5

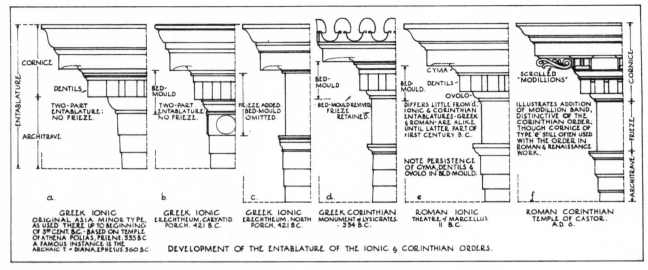

Figure 2. *Development of the entablature of the Ionic and Corinthian orders.*

them, their bases corresponding in level with the foot of the lower Doric colonnade, and their heads with the capitals of the higher, thus affording a sightly linkage.

Whilst the Greek Doric and Ionic orders were evolved simultaneously from wooden prototypes, and always reflect their constructional origin, a third order, the Corinthian, owes its beginnings to an artificial, aesthetic impulse. Its invention is attributed to a Greek of the name Callimachus, a bronze worker of Corinth of the fifth century B.C. Whether or no the tradition is true, it appears that Corinth was the seat of its origin, and since Corinth was a famed centre of the bronze-working craft in ancient times, there is justification for the belief that the earliest expressions of the order were in bronze. The original invention applied only to the capital, rich with foliations based on plant forms, and even when translated from bronze into stone, the order was Ionic as regards the entablature and shaft. The Greeks seem scarcely to have recognised its identity as a separate order, since it is only rarely used, and even so, nearly always in conjunction with one or both of the older orders.

The earliest known architectural instance was inside the naos of the Temple of Apollo Epicurius c. 420 B.C. at Bassae, on the Greek mainland, where there was only a single column, sharing the same entablature as adjacent Ionic columns. This building was remarkable in many ways, for apart from an unusual arrangement of plan, it incorporated all three of the orders, Doric outside, and Ionic and Corinthian within. The Ionic capitals too are of unusual type (Plate 25). The architect, Ictinus, was also architect of the Parthenon, jointly with Callicrates. The Corinthian order similarly was used internally in three of the circular temples which occasionally are found—at Epidaurus, Delphi and Olympia.

The Corinthian order appears for the first time externally on the Monument of Lysicrates, Athens,

334 B.C. (Plate 37). The suggestion of a metallic origin for the Corinthian capital is strongly supported here by the apparent direct imitation of a bronze technique, evidenced in the tight crispness of the foliage and a series of " rosettes " between the acanthus leaves in all probability reproducing the pins which in the metallic original fastened the leaves to the core or " bell " of the capital. Yet, the entablature still is essentially Ionic in character. The three-part Ionic entablature by now customary in Athens and the Greek mainland is used, but with the original Asiatic bed-mould once more restored to the cornice (Figure 2, d). In this revised form, the entablature continues to serve for Ionic and Corinthian alike. The Corinthian entablature only received its distinguishing characteristic, the " modillion " band, at Roman hands, in the latter part of the first century B.C. (Figure 2, f). The great Temple of Jupiter Olympius at Athens (Plate 39), begun about 170 B.C. but completed from the designs of a Roman architect c. A.D. 130, serves to illustrate the inspiration for this order, so popular with the Romans, passing from Greece to Rome. The dentils have here become very large moulded blocks.

THE TUSCAN ORDER

All the above examples of Greek monumental architecture, except the last-named, which is transitional, belong to the " Hellenic " period, of which the earliest known remains date from about the eighth century B.C. Somewhat earlier, probably about the ninth century B.C., colonists from Lydia or Lycia in Asia Minor settled in the west-central part of Italy and founded Etruria, a state roughly corresponding in situation and area with the modern province of Tuscany. The Etruscans continuously maintained associations with the Greeks and developed a pale reflection of their architecture, but with marked advances in structural principle and method, due partly to their own virility and partly to national (Italian) influences. Their architecture perished in immaturity after Etruria was finally overwhelmed by the conquering Romans in 309 B.C. Their bequest to the Romans was the Tuscan order. Actually, in Etruscan times, this order had never been wholly translated into stone. Like the primitive Greek Ionic, the masonry columns supported a wooden entablature, protected and decorated with terra-cotta slabs. The space between the columns was very wide. The resemblance to the decadent Doric was so very close that the addition, in Roman times, of a stone entablature, with a consequent rearrangement of the column centering, made the two almost indistinguishable. In point of fact the Tuscan is nothing more than a simplified Roman Doric, and truly authentic examples of the complete order are non-existent in antiquity. Those occasionally cited may be equally well regarded as Doric with certain elements omitted. Its re-creation as a separate order is due to the Italian Renaissance architect-writers of the fifteenth and sixteenth centuries A.D., who based their individual versions upon a description by the Roman writer Vitruvius, who, however, speaks of timber for the entablature, and stone only for the columns.

THE ROMAN ORDERS

The Romans absorbed the Greek architectural tradition and ensured its continuance, though with modifications due firstly to their Etruscan heritage and secondly to their own constructional and inventive genius. In the earliest Roman monuments we find that those tendencies already observed in Greek architecture had been maintained. The elongation of the orders and the lightening of their entablatures, became even more marked. In other words the earliest monumental architecture of Rome is imitative of that of the latest phases of the Greek. But during the first century B.C. highly important developments took place. To the Greek orders there had been but two major parts, the column and the entablature, the columns standing usually, in temple architecture, upon a flight of a few steps. In the traditional Roman temple the floor occurred at a much higher level and the columns were raised upon a high platform known as a " podium ". This brought into common association with the Roman orders, a third part, the " pedestal ", not always present in every type of building, but extremely frequent. Another adjunct to the order proper was the " parapet ", a low wall which served, where necessary, to give protection to persons using a flat roof at the top level of the order, or merely to give additional decorative enrichment. Roman parapets usually were " blind ", i.e., built solidly of stone, though stiffened at regular intervals with sturdy, short posts. Like the pedestals, which in detail they closely resembled, the posts had a 'cap' moulding and a base (Plate A).

Still more important was the now almost universal use of the arch form, known to the Greeks, but rarely used by them architecturally. In Roman practice arched openings were regularly enframed by columns partially attached to the walls, sometimes standing upon pedestals. Under these new conditions, proportions were inevitably determined by the shape of the arch enclosed, and became a little less slender than sometimes they had been. Nevertheless the distinguishing features of the several orders remained unaltered. The Romans adopted both the Doric and the Ionic from the Greeks and developed the Corinthian. The Roman Doric, still the must sturdy of the three, had a height of column usually approximating to eight diameters, the Ionic nine, and the Corinthian ten, but these proportions were by no means regularly observed. Entablatures in general, no matter what the order, ranged between one-quarter and one-fifth the height of the column. The Roman Doric entablature consequently was much lighter than its Greek counterpart, and, most incongruously, the columns of the lighter orders carried the heavier entablatures, quite the reverse from the Greek. The quality of detail became much more coarse, and instead of the refined and delicate curves, approximating in profile to parabolas, hyperbolas and ellipses, the Roman mouldings took the cruder forms of the quadrant, semicircle or arc. Roman architecture is ornate, bold and grandiose when compared with the Greek. Even in the selection of materials there was much more ostentation. Coloured marbles were freely employed as a decoration to wall faces, and the shafts of columns often were coloured marble monoliths. In such cases the usual fluting was omitted in order to display the fine qualities of the material.

Though the Romans were more concerned to follow Greek ideas than to invent new parts for the orders, they had necessarily to adapt them to many new situations, for their buildings were far more elaborate than the simple structures of the Greeks, and much vaster in size. They were great builders, but indifferent artists. The admission of the arch form to the established range of architectural elements was not a matter of free choice but the direct and inescapable outcome of their brilliant advances in constructive technique. The Roman decorative problems were indeed far greater than their artistic ability to solve them, and they used the orders in many illogical ways. Columns were used not only in simple rhythms, but in coupled pairs or groups, or they were spaced at alternately wide and narrow intervals. Frequently, almost representatively, the orders were arranged in tiers, one series above another ; two, three and four stages high. Instead of running continuously, entablatures often were broken into wilful decorative features or thrown forward to match the vertical lines of attached columns below. Niches, framed in the orders, were a favourite mode of wall decoration.

The Roman Doric order lost a great deal of its popularity early in the period of the Roman Empire (Empire, 27 B.C. —A.D. 330) and subsequently the surviving instances of its use are principally those of the attached order, used in such buildings as amphitheatres and theatres, where the whole range of orders was used decoratively in superimposed tiers. The earliest examples naturally are transitional in character, partly Greek and partly Roman, as is shown in some particulars by the Theatre of Marcellus (11 B.C., Plate 12). Here the order still lacks a base, which feature, however, it eventually acquired under the influence of the Tuscan, as also a smooth "necking" at the top of the shaft. (Note—Unfortunately, none of the Roman examples given illustrates the developed Doric base.) In Roman practice there were two versions, the "Denticular", employing a row of dentils in the cornice similar to those of the Ionic, and the "Mutular", in which the cornice more closely approximates to the Greek original and includes the "mutules". (Note—The latter version is best illustrated here by the Renaissance order on Plate 18.)

In keeping with precedent, the Roman Ionic order remained moderately ornate. Apart from adjustments to the proportions of the cornice, involving a reduction in the size of the dentils, the changes were of a general nature. The projection of the volutes of the capital was much diminished and a plinth was regularly used with the "Attic" base (Plate 28). Like the Doric, this order was supplanted in popularity early in the Roman Empire by the Corinthian, the latter, in its luxuriance, appealing more strongly to the florid Roman taste.

The Corinthian order owed its full development as an independent order to the Romans. In Greek usage, as we have seen, the Corinthian was little more than a decorative variant of the Ionic, affecting the column capital and little else. The one kind of entablature served for both. The order was still in this incomplete form when the Romans began to employ it freely in the first century B.C. (see The Temple of Vesta, Tivoli, c. 80 B.C., Plate 41), but towards the end of that century an important innovation was made. A new member, known now as the "modillion band", was introduced at the top of the bed-mould of the cornice, from which regularly-spaced moulded blocks ("modillions") projected to give apparent support to the corona. Between the blocks, decorative "coffers" were sunk into the underside of the corona. A further development soon followed, converting the simple "block" modillions into a more elaborate scrolled form (Plate 42). The latter have come to be regarded as the proper counterpart of the developed Corinthian order, though in point of fact the Romans used the block or scrolled types indiscriminately, and even reverted at times to the original Ionic kind of cornice by omitting them altogether (see Temple of Antoninus and Faustina, A.D. 141; Plate 47). To accord with the ornate character of the capital, the Romans also added minor mouldings elsewhere and, as with all the orders, decorated the mouldings freely with too-profuse carved running ornament. Roman Corinthian capitals have rather more elaborate foliage than the Greek, and the leaves of the acanthus are broader and less spiky. One of the finest instances of the order, true to type, more restrained and better proportioned than most is that of the Temple of Castor and Pollux (A.D. 6, Plate 42).

The Romans devised yet another order, the "Composite", completing the full historical total of five, though they seem never to have finally settled what its proper components were to be. The Renaissance architects, much later on, were more systematic in allotting each order its due and appropriate parts and in fixing a gradation of decorative importance rising from the austerely simple Tuscan at the one extreme, through Doric, Ionic and Corinthian to the ultimate Composite, the most pretentious of them all. In Roman hands the Composite order was precisely what the term suggests, an assemblage of elements already in use as parts of one or other of the older orders. The inspiration is probably again Greek, for possible precedents for the capital, at least, are not lacking in Greek Hellenistic architecture. The general proportions of the order were similar to those of the Corinthian, and always remain so in later historical practice down to modern times. The distinguishing feature is, of course, the capital, and in effect this is a combination of the Ionic scrolled volutes with the lower, foliated parts of the Corinthian capital (Plate 55). The column base, like that of the Corinthian, is recognisably Attic, still comparable with the Ionic type despite small additional mouldings sometimes used in an endeavour to sustain its superior decorative pretensions. Whatever the principle may have been, in actual practice the old Attic base, with minor variations or additions, served the Ionic, Corinthian and Composite orders indiscriminately. The entablatures apparently were interchangeable too, save that the modillion band was never used with the Ionic. With each of these three orders, the foundation in the original Ionic remains plainly apparent. For the Corinthian and Composite the modillion band might or might not be present, and it was a matter of artistic whim in each case whether the block or the scrolled variety of modillions was to be used. Of the three Roman instances illustrated in the body of this book (Plates 55, 56, 57) two of the entablatures bear scrolled modillions and have profiles quite indistinguishable from Corinthian, whilst the third is to all intents and purposes Ionic, having all the main parts proper to that order and no modillion band or other distinguishing feature whatever to determine its identity as a separate and more elaborate order. Identifying the Composite order by the capital alone, it first comes into use about the middle of the first century A.D., and the earliest example in Rome is that to which incidental reference has just been made; on the Arch of Titus, A.D. 82 (Plate 55).

THE RENAISSANCE ORDERS

Each successive phase of Classic Architecture seems to have produced its complement of architect-writers. Stimulated by pride of achievement, these practical-minded authors have endeavoured to clarify contemporary thought and ideals, and to record for posterity the code of rules to be observed in the production of good architecture. Ictinus, joint architect of the Parthenon, wrote a book on the completed monument. This book has not survived, neither has that of Hermogenes, written about the middle of the second century B.C., prescribing a code of proportions for the Ionic order, though it is known that the latter work was frequently consulted by Roman architects and that both were known to the all-important Roman author, Vitruvius, living in the latter part of the first century B.C. Indeed, in so far as the orders are concerned, the books of Vitruvius were almost wholly based upon the work of earlier Greek writers. Vitruvius is important not so much for the quality of his writings on the subject, but by reason of the fact that his treatise alone still existed at the commencement of that revival of Roman architecture, the " Renaissance " (A.D. 1420). His work in its turn supplied the inspiration to a succession of first Italian, then French and finally English writers upon the Orders of Architecture. The most outstanding of these were Palladio (1518-80) and Vignola (1507-73), and the somewhat less celebrated Alberti, Scamozzi and Serlio among the Italians, and De Lorme, Lescot and Goujon among the French. By them the codification of the orders was carried to much greater lengths than hitherto. Vitruvius was certainly their inspiration, but little more. Each rigorously and exhaustively measured, observed and noted the details of surviving Roman monuments and drew up a standard of proportions and parts in accordance with his individual views. The " Five Renaissance Orders " each acquired a definite and characteristic form. Never had their identity been so completely established in Roman days, and certainly none found a wholly complete foundation of fact in antiquity. What Rome failed to produce the Renaissance imagination supplied. Each order must be so complete as to meet their every modern circumstance. Each order must have three main parts, entablature, column and pedestal. Each must be capable of application as a free standing order or attached and enframing an arch, and a regulation spacing of column for either arrangement must be devised. There must be a standard " impost " mould from which the arch might spring, a standard archivolt and a standard pilaster to " respond " to the column. For the greater part of these details, historical precedent already existed, but such was the variety exhibited by the Roman remains that the process of selection must have indeed been difficult. Full coherence can only have been secured by the exercise of a healthy imagination. But whilst complete justification for each and every part of the Renaissance orders may be lacking, the spirit of antiquity is invariably admirably caught. The inventions are remarkably adept and do no small honour to the traditions of ancient Rome. Furthermore, these " moderns " were moved by a true artistic impulse and exercised a critical and selective faculty which strongly distinguished their architectural capacities from those of the Romans. The Renaissance architects in some measure recovered the æsthetic ideals of the Greeks and imbued the borrowed elements with a vitality the Romans had never been able to impart.

The social system changed considerably in the thousand or so years which separated the Renaissance from the Ancient Roman civilization. Buildings were no longer ponderously vast, but compact in bulk and light in structure. The imperialistic Romans had made enormous strides in developing arcuated construction, buttressing arches with massive masonry ; in the Italian Renaissance light-shelled buildings of an intimate social character

often were bound together with iron or wooden ties. The architecture of the two cultures could not fail to be essentially different, despite the Renaissance passionate endeavour to recover the Roman decorative system. None of the Roman practices escaped Renaissance attention, but devotion to presumed Roman ideals restrained Renaissance architects from deliberately attempting to add to the tally of the time-honoured orders and attendant elements. Nevertheless, some progression was in the circumstances inevitable, and some few new developments were made.

Figure 3. Development of the Renaissance balustrade.

Roman parapets had solid panels between the strengthening posts, or they were sculptured or pierced with patterns (Figure 3). In later mediaeval and early Renaissance times in Italy, the parapets often were treated as tiny colonnades, with the panels filled with miniature Doric, Ionic or other columns supporting the upper protective rail. About the year 1476, an important innovation was made in north-west Italy. The shafts of the miniature columns were shaped to a skittle-like profile, in the representative case, slenderly waisted in the upper part and bulbous in the lower. Thus was born the true baluster, and the term " balustrade " henceforward became an apt description of any parapet with this feature. Further experiments of treatment were made, but balusters nearly always retain an obvious resemblance to the column of the order—usually Tuscan or Doric—from which they derived.

Another typical Renaissance usage is that known fittingly as the " Renaissance " arcade. The Greeks did not use the arch in their æsthetic system : the Romans enframed it between pairs of columns and their entablature. In this new arrangement (there are rare Roman precedents) arches stand actually upon the capitals of a range of columns, the latter sometimes spaced singly, sometimes in pairs. (Plate E, Figures B and D.) A combination of the Renaissance with the Roman form of arcade gave another now famous device—the so-called

"Palladian motif". (Plate E, Figure D.)

Not less important to the future of architecture was the use of " rustication " deliberately for effect, in which rough-cut or texturally-tooled stones are placed astride the shafts of columns or introduced into the entablature of orders otherwise fully carved in the ordinary way. The practice was initiated in north-east Italy in the early sixteenth century as an extension of methods used in Italy in the decorative rustication of wall surfaces since later mediaeval days. The few Roman precedents for the rustication of the orders proper appear to be accidental, and due merely to incompletion. Rustication is a sophistication which became vastly important in Renaissance architecture; but a fuller investigation of the various devices used is outside the scope of this book.

Renaissance architects were much more systematic in their decorative methods than the Romans had been. They used the orders rationally and investigated all practicable combinations and permutations of them and their adjuncts. They devised fixed composite arrangements or " motifs ", applicable not as so many parts but as a whole. The Palladian motif referred to above was one of these, in which larger and smaller sized orders are interwoven; but there were several other types of standardized arcade as well as of colonnade, window and doorway surround. The writings on the orders of architecture were not alone concerned to set forth the due parts and proportions of each of the five orders, but also gave diagrams explaining the rules for the use of the orders and their adjuncts for various decorative ends. The nature of these systems will be shown in the next section.

GENERAL NOTES ON THE PLATES

INTRODUCTORY PLATES

Method of Drawing the Orders

IN addition to Normand's drawings, seven introductory plates are supplied of which plates A to D show methods by which the principal parts and proportions of the orders can be committed to memory for the purposes of rapid drawing and design. Subsequently, the details may be filled out, according to individual choice, from the alternatives among the ancient and Renaissance examples detailed in the body of the volume.

The older, cumbersome method of expressing the proportions of the orders in terms of modules and partes (see below) was outmoded by the system originated, so far as Britain is concerned, by James Gibbs and published in 1732, by which any dimension adopted for the total height of an order may be progressively subdivided into parts until even the smallest elements are allocated to their appropriate position. His system is much the better adapted to the visual memory possessed by most trained architects and artists but, paradoxically, has yet the defect of being too meticulously complete. No special stress is laid upon the relative proportions of the several orders.

Professor William R. Ware, whose work, " The American Vignola ", was published in 1902, mitigates this defect. He elucidates the principal relations between the orders in terms of multiples or duodecimal fractions of a unit lower diameter, then proceeding to subdivision of the major elements on similar lines to Gibbs. Additionally, both authors demonstrate useful geometrical correspondences.

In the plates here published, the general proportions employed in previous works of Renaissance and later dates have been amended to conform with current opinion as to the respective æsthetic functions of the major parts of the orders. Entablatures are shown progressively shallower and more delicate in detail as their attendant columns become the more slender and graceful. Pedestals are made to show the qualities of the order to which they belong, being, in the case of the Tuscan, squat, stable and strong, and at the other extreme affording an easy transition from the swift verticality of the Corinthian or Composite shaft to the horizontal lines of the ground or immediate substructure. Parapets, termed balustrades when balusters are incorporated, bear a regular relation to the height of the entablature in each case. Incidentally, it should be stressed that neither parapets nor pedestals are an inseparable part of an order and, for the purpose of relating an actual building to the human scale, may suitably be varied from the given proportions when occasion demands.

Three parallel systems of establishing the proportions are employed, the one overlapping and confirming the other. In Plate A, the sizes of the main elements are shown in terms of the full lower diameter, which serves as the unit. First subdivisions of such elements are shown on the same plate, and the chief geometrical relations are stressed by means of dotted lines, these always at 45 degrees if not either vertical or horizontal.

The three plates following, Plates B to D, review the orders severally, including the two alternative versions of the Doric. On the left-hand side of the plate each is shown comprehensively, except that the central part of the column shaft is omitted, whilst on the right details are given at three times the scale of the latter. The system of progressive subdivision of parts and that by which geometrical relations are illustrated by 45-degree, horizontal and vertical lines, here predominate, but also, reference is included to the main proportions in terms of the lower diameter of the column shaft.

The control exercised over the spacing of columns by the triglyphs, dentils or modillions occurring in the entablatures should be especially noted. In each case one should fall on the centre line of any supporting column. Hence Doric columns should be spaced in multiples of one and a quarter diameters, Ionic in multiples of one-eighth of a diameter and Corinthian and Composite in multiples of seven-twelfths of a diameter.

Application of the Orders

FOR all that the orders and their adjuncts are capable of producing so large a variety of differing designs, all practicable compositions are based upon one or other of a relatively small number of fundamental arrangements. We have seen that there are but five orders, Tuscan, Doric, Ionic, Corinthian and Composite—stated in advancing order of decorative interest—each comprising two main parts ; column and entablature. The regular adjuncts are the pilaster, pedestal, parapet, and elements of the arch.

Proceeding from this point we note as a preliminary that an order may be expressed as normally free-standing, or in decorative relation to a wall. In the latter case the columns may be attached to the wall, with three-quarters of the diameter projecting therefrom, or pilasters may be used instead. A fourth alternative is that the columns should stand near to the wall, but have pilaster responds immediately behind them. The latter three alternatives are illustrated in plan on Plate G, Figures E 1, 2 and 3. This range of alternative expressions of an order should be borne in mind in relation to each of the systems defined below. Incidentally, it should be said here that the shafts of pilasters should not diminish in diameter from bottom to top, and they should not have entasis. To avoid a clumsy effect the width of pilasters should be one-twelfth less than the normal diameter for comparable columns.

Columns spaced systematically apart, crowned by their entablature, constitute a "colonnade". The columns may be spaced singly at regular intervals, or in pairs at regular intervals or again, at alternately wide and narrow intervals. For convenience these may be called 'Regular', 'Coupled' and 'Alternating' forms of colonnade spacing. (Plate E, Figure A.) Every colonnade must be based upon one of these alternatives, for there are no others, though it is practicable to interweave a smaller version of one of them with a larger version of the same or another. The spacing of columns in a colonnade is determined by two considerations : first that the interval shall be a multiple of the spacing of triglyphs, modillions or even dentils in the cornice, one of these elements to lie always above the axis of a column ; and second that the actual dimensions of the colonnade shall be such as to allow free unimpeded passage between the bases of the columns. In general in the use of the orders, it should be kept in mind that the simpler orders convey a grave air, and the more ornate a lighter if more graceful impression. Subtleties of elegance may be contrived by using more slender proportions than normal, the entablature being lightened in sympathy with the degree of slenderness of the columns. Any colonnade or arcade will look trivial at too small an actual size in relation to the human form and, up to a point, all will improve in impressiveness as their dimensions increase. When very large, the simpler orders will look majestic indeed, whilst the more ornate may seem a trifle coarse.

The decorative possibilities of the colonnade may be further extended by the introduction of pedestals under each of the columns, or these may be connected by "blind" panels or by balustrades. Alternatively or additionally, blind or balustraded parapets may be used at the upper level.

Arcades offer more basic alternative arrangements than colonnades. The "Simple" arcade (Plate E, Figure C) is merely a regular series of openings in a wall, the full order not appearing at all. The archivolts spring from impost mouldings which serve to connect the arches, the profile of both of these features being selected to accord with the character of the entablature used to crown the wall. Sometimes this upper entablature may be simplified by omitting architrave and frieze, or an "astragal cornice" is used, the astragal being a simple torus mould with fillet below, serving to demarcate a frieze and thus relate the crowning cornice sympathetically to the wall from which it springs. The arches may have a plain or decorated keystone at their head, as is the case in any type of arcade.

The "Roman" arcade has been referred to frequently before. In this arrangement, the arches are enframed in the chosen order (Tuscan, Doric, etc.) which itself may be expressed in pilastered form or as attached columns. As the order is actually present the dimensions are related to the lower diameter of the shaft of the order in the usual way. A well-proportioned opening will be approximately twice as high as wide, but the degree of flexibility is limited by the aesthetic necessity of ensuring that the columns or pilasters lie in line with triglyphs, modillions or dentils in the cornice, when any of these are present. The diagrams on Plate E, Figure D 1, 2 and 3, illustrate typical arrangements. From these it will be seen that besides the simpler system in which the columns or pilasters are spaced singly, the latter may be arranged in pairs or in alternately wide and narrow spacings as in the case of the colonnade. These may therefore be designated similarly as the 'Regular', 'Coupled' and 'Alternating' versions of the Roman arcade.

In the case of the alternating arrangement, niche recesses or minor openings commonly were fitted between the lesser spacings. A single unit of the alternating version of the Roman arcade, flanked by the minor intercolumniations, when standing independently often is known as the "triumphal arch" motif, on account of its close resemblance to the disposition of the orders in the Roman typical triumphal arch.

It is scarcely necessary to say that with the Roman arcade also, pedestals may be used under the columns (or pilasters) and that they may be joined together, as before, by blind panels or balustrades. Or again, that plain or balustraded parapets may be added, if desired.

The "Renaissance" arcade, a very light and graceful affair, hardly capable of expressing dignified severity however it may be used, is one in which the arches spring actually from the column tops. It has the three variants, 'Regular', 'Coupled', and 'Alternating', as before (Plate E, Figures B 1, 2 and 3). The arches should not be less than about fifteen to twenty feet high (five to seven metres) or the motif loses most of its charm. The springing of the arches should fall at about two-thirds up the height. The difficult matter is to ensure that the archivolts are firmly seated upon the column caps, and often they are made to intersect at this point (Plate 69). Also, the arcade must be firmly buttressed at the extremities; though it was the Renaissance practice to tie the arches together with metal bars at their springing. Pedestals may be used with any one of the variants of the type, but with caution since they introduce weakness in effect as well as fact in an already fragile arrangement. Heavy crowning entablatures too are unsuitable, and often these are simplified by the omission of certain of the usual mouldings. Similar considerations arise if parapets are applied, the cap and base mouldings of this adjunct being reduced to their simplest terms.

The "Palladian" arcade is actually a combination of two of the more elementary types, a colonnade at large scale interpenetrated by a smaller scale arcade of the Renaissance alternating type. It again has the three variants, 'Regular', 'Coupled', and 'Alternating', this classification being determined by the larger columns (Plate E, Figures E 1, 2 and 3). The bays or units are exceptionally wide in relation to their height, which makes the type very convenient on certain occasions. The panels or "spandrils" at the sides of the arches may be variously treated, though usually they are pierced, as shown, by small roundels to suggest lightness, in view of the relative frailty of the supporting small columns. The latter have to be doubled in the depth of the wall, as otherwise they would provide insufficient bearing area. In this Palladian type, too, it would not look sightly or safe if the entablature were to span the wide bays in the ordinary direct way, projecting as it would to the same extent as the principal columns or pilasters. Hence it is broken back to the main wall face on each side of the columns or pilasters of the main order. Pedestals are a practicable addition, once again, and parapets, blind or balustraded, are more or less normal, as they help to consolidate the rather loose appearance due to the variety of the elements incorporated in the motif, and the wide bay proportions.

Though it may seem remarkable, the few types reviewed above are the full tally of the classical primary motifs. Extension is practicable only by combinations; not forgetting that large and small scale versions, even of the same type, may be interwoven to form composite motifs.

There is, however, one adjunct to the orders which latterly has not been mentioned—the pediment. We saw that this originated in a structural arrangement over the ends of Greek temples, but was soon turned to less specific decorative account. Its æsthetic function is to embrace and unify local compositions of the architectural elements; colonnades, porticoes, gateways and door and window surrounds. Problems arise as to the correct angle of slope to be used on different occasions. The views of Vitruvius and the Italian Renaissance architect Serlio on the subject are expressed in the diagrams shown in Plate 65, but each of these methods has the demerit that it takes no account of the proportions of the feature to which the

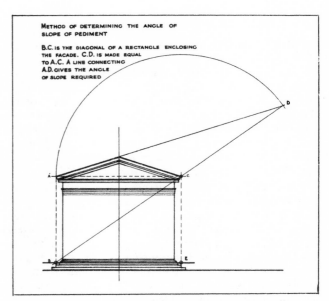

Figure 4. Method of determining the slope of pediments.

pediment relates, being based solely upon the width. Figure 4 shows a more logical if equally empirical rule. Supposing a portico or similar feature to be represented by the rectangle ABCE, a diagonal is projected to a point D, BC and CD being made equal. A line joining A and D then gives the correct angle of slope.

In Greek Doric practice, the "raking" cornices of a pediment did not reproduce the mutules which figured in the horizontal cornice at the base, though they, comprised mouldings which in true section had an otherwise precisely similar profile. In Renaissance usage, horizontal and raking cornices were treated alike. Elements such as mutules, modillions and dentils occurred in the raking cornices at points immediately above their counterparts in the horizontal cornice, but their sides were kept perpendicular. The half-pediment shown in Figure E, Plate G, illustrates the principle.

In Hellenistic Greek, in Roman and Renaissance architecture, pediments were often used inconsequently, without any great regard for their constructive origin, to serve decorative needs. Sometimes the apex and the greater part of the adjoining raking cornices was omitted altogether, and the free ends of the latter stopped short in 'return' moulds or perhaps turned into scrolls. Segmentally-shaped pediments came to be a popular alternative to the original triangular kind and were subject to similar wayward variations.

In the classical decorative system, doors, windows, niches and other similar local features almost invariably were enriched by moulded architectural surrounds. Some famous ancient instances, mostly Roman, are shown on Plate 60 and others of Renaissance date, very richly ornate, on Plate 61. Windows do not often occur in Greek temple buildings, as the main apartment was relatively small and such natural light as was needed on ceremonial occasions could be admitted through the open doors of the great portal. Roman and Renaissance doorways were usually more elaborate than the Greek, at times to the point of including the entire order in the enframement.

It is the purpose of the introductory Plates F and G to illustrate the various types schematically, in ascending order of elaboration. There are square-headed and round-headed kinds, though only the first group is included here, leaving the round-headed series to be deduced by inference. The diagrams in each instance illustrate doorways, but the simpler types at least would serve for windows and niches too, with little modification.

The simplest architectural treatment is that with a moulded architrave surrounding three sides of the opening, finishing at the foot either on a plinth block or by " returning " the moulding in the way shown (Plate F, Figure A). In this form the enframement represents a direct translation into stone of the timber baulks which had formed the jambs and lintol of the doorways of the early Greek temples, when the latter had had timber-framed walls. The original material is still more strongly suggested when the lintol projects a little on each side of the jambs, producing an arrangement now known as a " crossette " (Plate F, Figures A 1 and 2). The double crossette (Figure A 3) is a Renaissance elaboration. The profile of the architrave moulding usually is identical with that proper to the similar element in the entablature of one or other of the orders, the selection being made according to the degree of elaboration required.

The next step in progressive enrichment is the addition of a cornice (Plate F, Figures B, B 1, B 3) simplified by the omission of a number of the normal constituent mouldings so that it may not look disproportionately heavy. Sometimes, no more than a cymatium is added as a capping to a straightforward architrave surround. Figures B 2 and B 4 show the method of relating a cornice to the architrave with crossette. The Figure C and its variants (Plate F) illustrate the use of a whole entablature at the head of the opening. The proportions, however, are not quite the same as in an ordinary entablature, for to avoid a clumsy effect, the cornice and frieze are reduced in size relative to the architrave. This adjustment again requires the omission of certain elements from the bed-mould of the cornice. At will, a triangular or segmental pediment may be added to the cornice, whether or no crossettes are employed.

Plate G shows departures of a more complex kind. Figure D illustrates a double enframement, the inner similar to that of the last type, the outer consisting of a pair of scrolled " consoles ", rising from additional " chambranle " strips adjacent to the jamb architraves to give support to the corona of the crowning cornice. At this stage of doorway enrichment quite a few minor variations are practicable, as one may see from the many actual instances of the type produced by celebrated architects of the Italian Renaissance. The internationally famous Vignola (1507-73) designed several which came almost to be universally accepted as standard composite motifs. One or two of these are illustrated on Plate 68. The type may readily be used with pediments, triangular or segmental, and with crossettes.

Type E on Plate G indicates, finally, how the full-dress order may be employed to give exceptionally rich effect to a doorway surround. It is at this stage of elaboration that the colonnade motif is called into service, either in its ' Regular ', ' Coupled ' or ' Alternating ' forms. The principles of use are those already enumerated, and illustrated on Plate E, Figure A. The diagrams on Plate G show how the conjunction is effected; and the part-plans there (E 1, 2 and 3) serve as a reminder that there is latitude to treat the full order either as a portico or as a more local surround decorating the wall in which the door actually occurs. There is latitude, too, to employ the customary adjuncts to the orders; pedestals below the columns; parapets, balustrades or triangular or segmental pediments above.

Though the parallel range of round-headed finishes to door and other wall openings is not attempted here, it will be clear that, apart from simple types in which the arch is employed as an integral part of the immediate surround of the opening, units of the arcade motifs shown diagrammatically on Plate E, each are capable of use for the superior grades of enrichment in their class.

ORIGINAL PLATES

FOR convenience of comparison and reference, the plates are arranged in five sections, each treating of one of the orders. The Tuscan, being the strongest and most simple, is taken first and the remainder follow in succession according to the decorative character they express; Doric, Ionic, Corinthian, Composite. Chronological sequence is not attempted.

The Tuscan order is represented only by the versions of the Renaissance authors, since there are no authentic examples existing in antiquity. Doric, Ionic, and Corinthian are illustrated by examples from all three periods, though the Greek Corinthian shows an incomplete development of the order. The Composite, being a Roman invention, not fully mature until the Renaissance, has no Greek illustrations.

It will be seen from a glance at the frontispiece that the monuments from which a large number of the plates are drawn vary tremendously in size. Actual dimensions in metres or feet would therefore be of little practical value for purposes of detailed comparison, and extremely inconvenient to use if the orders are to serve the purposes of modern design. Hence their several proportions are usually expressed in terms of the lower diameter of the column. In any order the lower diameter of the column is presumed to equal two " modules ", each module being conveniently divided into thirty " partes ". All other dimensions can then be expressed in these terms, and any two examples can be immediately compared no matter what their actual size. Some such system was, of course, essential to the architect-authors of the Renaissance, whose empirical codes of proportions, illustrated herein, have no material existence, in order that they might usefully serve their intended purpose and apply commonly to projected buildings, no matter what the size. Then again, since the object of the inclusion of the antique examples in this book is very much the same, the extension of the system to them also is scarcely less necessary. Each plate, therefore, except the last, is dimensioned in modules and parts, and for additional convenience a scale is included at the foot of the page.

Most of the classic monuments are now in ruins and it is not always possible to establish the original proportions with exactitude. Decorative details frequently survive even when the remainder of the building has almost wholly disappeared, but even these are occasionally in a very mutilated state. Capitals are particularly prone to damage, especially in respect of projecting leaves and volutes. In such cases it has been necessary to make small restorations based on such information as survives. Particularly in Roman buildings, the original setting out is sometimes inaccurate and the carving of running mouldings and decoration is extremely crude, the dimensions varying at different points. Discrepancies of this nature can only be overcome by an approximation, which has been carried out with a due regard to the character of the order as a whole.

The Greek orders consist only of entablature and column. The column stands upon a " crepidoma " (often termed " stylobate ") of three steps. The " respond " to the column is the " anta ", which usually has a cap and base quite different from those of the column.

The Roman orders, when free standing, have usually only two parts, entablature and column, but a pedestal is sometimes included. The respond to the column is the " pilaster ", the design of its capital shaft and base closely following those of the column. The Roman orders, when attached, generally enframe an arch, and may stand upon pedestals. The details included in the plates will vary according to the circumstances of the monument illustrated.

The Renaissance orders are designed for use with or without the pedestal, whether free standing, or attached and enclosing an arch. A spacing for the columns of an ordinary colonnade is given, but others can be devised according to the interval of decorative elements in the entablature, i.e., triglyphs, dentils or modillions. (Note.— The spacing of elements in the entablature with respect to column centerings was disregarded in Roman monuments.) Details of impost and archivolt mouldings are supplied for use with the arcaded order, and the essential dimensions for the setting out of the arch are shown alternatively with or without the pedestal. The respond to the column is the pilaster, which is similar in design to the column.

With the Renaissance orders, as with the Roman, the entablature usually bears a regular relation to the column height no matter what the order used. Thus the more slender orders carry the heavier weights; an illogical arrangement. Palladio and Scamozzi generally proportioned their entablatures in the ratio of one-fifth. Vignola always used the quarter. Vitruvius devised a means of regulating the proportions of the entablature in accordance with the height of the column, the proportion increasing with the size. This is shown on Plate 59.

One important difference between Greek and other orders should be noted. The Greek entablature usually projects beyond (i.e. overhangs) the upper diameter of the column shaft, whereas in Roman and Renaissance orders the main face of the entablature, normally, continues vertically the line of the silhouette of the diminished upper shaft.

In all periods, the entablature consists of three parts, cornice, frieze and architrave, except the early form of Greek Ionic, which excludes the frieze.

The column normally has three parts, capital, shaft and base, but there is no base to the Greek Doric and none to the early form of the Roman Doric.

The pedestal or the parapet, when present, have three parts; cap, die and base.

DESCRIPTIVE NOTES ON THE PLATES

INTRODUCTORY PLATES

Simplified method of drawing the Renaissance orders. The main proportions are expressed in terms of the lower diameter (D) of the column, and the mouldings then are determined by sub-division.

Plate A. Typical Mouldings. Comparison of the principal proportions of the orders.

Plate B. The Tuscan and Doric (Mutular) orders.

Plate C. The Doric (Denticular) and Ionic orders.

Plate D. The Corinthian and Composite orders.

Plate E. Types of colonnade and arcade.

Plate F. Door openings, simple types.

Plate G. Door openings, double and compound types.

ORIGINAL PLATES

Comprising actual examples taken from ancient Greek and Roman buildings, and standardised versions of each of the orders as compiled by famous Italian and French Renaissance Architects. The proportions throughout are expressed in terms of modules and partes. A module is equal to one-half of the lower diameter of the column and there are thirty partes in a module.

Frontispiece. Ancient Greek and Roman examples, included in the plates following, shown comparatively at their actual dimensions.

Plate 1. TUSCAN. RENAISSANCE. The order according to Palladio (1518-1580).

Plate 2. TUSCAN. RENAISSANCE. The order according to Scamozzi (1551-1616).

Plate 3. TUSCAN. RENAISSANCE. The order according to Serlio (c. 1475-1555).

Plate 4. TUSCAN. RENAISSANCE. The order according to Vignola (1507-1573).

Plate 5. DORIC. GREEK. Parthenon, Athens, 447-432 B.C. The finest expression of the fully developed order.

Plate 6. DORIC. GREEK. The Temple of Apollo Epicurius, Bassae, c. 420 B.C. This unusual building is Doric externally, but has ten Ionic and one Corinthian column inside the naos. (*See Plate* 25.)

Plate 7. DORIC. GREEK. The " Theseum " (a temple probably of Hephaestus), Athens, 421 B.C. The proportions are less satisfactory than those of the Parthenon, the columns being more slender and the entablature heavier.

Plate 8. DORIC. GREEK. The Temple of Poseidon, Paestum, c. 450 B.C. The heavy proportions illustrate its early date.

Plate 9. DORIC. GREEK. Three examples : (*a*) Temple of Apollo, Delos, c. 475 and later. There occurred a long break in the building of this temple and it was not, even so, completed. The flutes on the shaft of the column were never carved. It was customary to carve the upper and lower portions before erection and the remainder *in situ*. (*b*) Portico of Philip of Macedon, Delos. A late example. The column shaft is very slender and the projection of the abacus slight. Compare (*c*) Temple of Apollo, Corinth, c. 535 B.C., where the swelling echinus projects boldly. The diminution of the column shaft here is considerable.

Plate 10. DORIC. GREEK. Various capitals : (*a*) Portico of Augustus, Athens ; (*b*) Propylea, Athens, 437 B.C. ; (*c*) Basilica, 540 B.C. and (*d*) Temple of Ceres, c. 530 B.C., Paestum. The gorge necking in these two examples is exceptional. Also, two other early examples found at Paestum.

Plate 11. DORIC. GREEK. Choragic Monument of Thrasyllus, Athens, 320 B.C.

Plate 12. DORIC. ROMAN. Theatre of Marcellus, 11 B.C. Showing the " Denticular " order in the later stages of transition from the Greek. There is still no base, but all other details are developed Roman.

Plate 13. DORIC. ROMAN. From details discovered at Albano, near Rome. The date is roughly that of the preceding example. The order is " Mutular ", but some of the entablature details are unorthodox.

Plate 14. DORIC. ROMAN. Thermae of Diocletian, Rome, A.D. 306. A late and somewhat coarse example of the " Denticular " order. The absence of a base at this period is exceptional.

Plate 15. DORIC. RENAISSANCE. The order according to Palladio. The mutules are expressed as sunk panels under the soffit of the corona.

Plate 16. DORIC. RENAISSANCE. The Denticular order according to Scamozzi. The impost and archivolt for this order are shown on Plate 19.

Plate 17. DORIC. RENAISSANCE. The Denticular order according to Vignola. The only Renaissance example without the full attic base.

Plate 18. DORIC. RENAISSANCE. The Mutular order according to Vignola.

Plate 19. DORIC. RENAISSANCE. The order according to Viala or Zannini, c. 1629. The treatment of the mutules resembles Palladio's. Also, according to De Lorme (Fr. c. 1515-1570), a simplified version.

Plate 20. IONIC. GREEK. Temple on the Ilissus, c. 450 B.C., showing the Attic version of the order, with a frieze.

Plate 21. IONIC. GREEK. Details of the Temple on the Ilissus illustrating the typical Greek method of treatment of volutes of the angle column and a method of setting out the volute.

Plate 22. IONIC. GREEK. Erechtheum, Athens, c. 421 B.C. North Porch. Usually regarded as the finest example of the Greek Ionic. Unlike the original Asiatic type of the order, this Athenian version includes a frieze.

Plate 23. IONIC. GREEK. Details from the North Porch of the Erechtheum, Athens, c. 421 B.C. (*See Note above.*)

Plate 24. IONIC. GREEK. Details from the Erechtheum, Athens, c. 421 B.C. (Normand describes these as from the Temple of Minerva Polias and the Erechtheum. Actually both are from the Erechtheum. The upper details are those of the west facade, which is an attached order, and the lower are those of the east portico. Both have the same entablature, which runs right round the building and is similar to that of the North Porch on Plate 22. The proportion for the entablature is—west facade, 2.41 ; east portico, 2.18.)

Plate 25. IONIC. GREEK. The Temple of Apollo Epicurius, Bassae, c. 420 B.C. The temple has north-south orientation instead of the usual east-west, and includes instances of all three of the Greek orders : Doric, Ionic, and Corinthian. The Ionic order is internal. See Plate 6 for the external Doric order.

Plate 26. IONIC. GREEK. The Temple of Minerva (Athena) Polias, Priene, c. 335 B.C. and later. This plate incorrectly shows a frieze to the entablature of the order. The correct arrangement is shown in Figure 2 a. In Asia Minor, where the Ionic order originated, a frieze was not regularly incorporated in the entablature before the third century B.C. A capital from this temple is shown also on Plate 27.

Plate 27. IONIC. GREEK. Various capitals : (*a*) Temple of Apollo Didyma, Miletus, c. 330 B.C. ; (*b*) Minerva Polias, Priene, c. 335 B.C. ; (*c*) Aqueduct of Hadrian, Athens. All illustrate the later type of Greek Ionic capital, the last being " transitional " to Roman character.

Plate 28. IONIC. ROMAN. Temple of Fortuna Virilis, Rome, c. 40 B.C. An early Roman example but already very ornate.

Plate 29. IONIC. ROMAN. Theatre of Marcellus, Rome, 11 B.C. The order is attached and occurs in the second tier. The column is unfluted.

Plate 30. IONIC. ROMAN. Thermæ of Diocletian, Rome, A.D. 306. A pilaster is shown in place of the column. The entablature illustrates typical late Roman practice. Note the " pulvinated " frieze.

Plate 31. IONIC. RENAISSANCE. The order according to Palladio. There are no dentils, but blocks are introduced into the cornice.

Plate 32. IONIC. RENAISSANCE. The order according to Scamozzi. The impost and archivolt to the order are shown on Plate 34. Scamozzi also uses blocks in the cornice but includes an uncut dentil mould. The disconnection of the volutes of the capitals repeats a late Roman practice.

Plate 33. IONIC. RENAISSANCE. The order according to Vignola. Probably the finest of the Renaissance series. The frieze decoration is based on that of the Roman Temple of Antoninus and Faustina. (*See Plate* 47.)

Plate 34. IONIC. RENAISSANCE. The order according to Serlio and Alberti (1404-1472). The latter uses an uncut dentil mould and a plain shaft.

Plate 35. IONIC. RENAISSANCE. Methods of drawing Ionic volutes according to (*a*) Palladio, (*b*) Vignola.

Plate 36. IONIC. RENAISSANCE. Methods of drawing Ionic volutes according to (*a*) D'Aviler, (*b*) Goldmann.

Plate 37. CORINTHIAN. GREEK. Monument of Lysicrates, Athens, 334 B.C. The first example of the order as used externally. The entablature is similar to developed Greek Ionic.

Plate 38. CORINTHIAN. GREEK. The Tower of the Winds, Athens, c. 50 B.C. The capitals are of unusual design, but for convenience, the order is classified as Corinthian. The structure was octagonal and accommodated a water-clock and sundials, and had a weather vane at the apex. The columns were part of two small porches at the base of the tower.

Plate 39. CORINTHIAN. GRAECO-ROMAN. Temple of Jupiter Olympius, Athens, c. 170 B.C. to c. A.D. 180. Finished from the designs of a Roman architect. The order is seen in process of development. Blocks were introduced into the cornice. The moulds of the base of the column overhang the line of the die of the pedestal, a feature of the early Roman orders.

Plate 40. CORINTHIAN. GRAECO-ROMAN. Two " transitional " examples : (*a*) Incantada, Salonica ; (*b*) Arch of Theseus, Athens. Probably erected by the Emperor Hadrian or his successor. The order is from the upper of two tiers.

Plate 41. CORINTHIAN. ROMAN. The Temple of Vesta, Tivoli, near Rome, c. 80 B.C. An early Roman instance of the Corinthian order. The profile of the entablature is similar to that of the contemporary Ionic, as the characteristic modillions had not yet been invented.

Plate 42. CORINTHIAN. ROMAN. Temple of Castor and Pollux, Rome, A.D. 6. (Normand erroneously described this temple as that of Jupiter Stator, of which a portion of the foundations only was recently discovered.) Probably the finest example of the Roman Corinthian.

Plate 43. CORINTHIAN. ROMAN. Temple of Vespasian, Rome, A.D. 80. The cornice is shown without its crowning " cymatium " moulding.

Plate 44. CORINTHIAN. ROMAN. The Pantheon, Rome, c. A.D. 120. The portico from which the order is taken may be earlier, viz. 27 B.C. The order is normal except that the dentils are uncut and the column is an unfluted monolith.

Plate 45. CORINTHIAN. ROMAN. The Pantheon, Rome, c. A.D. 120. The interior order. The upper part of the cornice is poorly proportioned. The dentils are again uncut.

Plate 46. CORINTHIAN. ROMAN. From the Forum of Nerva, c. A.D. 90-97. A normal example of the order but heavily decorated. The " corona ", in the upper part of the cornice, is much too small. The entablature carries a high attic (not shown on the plate) broken round the line of the column. The column was half-buried in the ground until recently. Hence a base is not given.

Plate 47. CORINTHIAN. ROMAN. Temple of Antoninus and Faustina, A.D. 141. Built during a brief period of revival of taste. Older forms and practices are consciously imitated. The modillions are suppressed and the dentils are uncut. A finely proportioned monument.

Plate 48. CORINTHIAN. ROMAN. Temple of Serapis, c. A.D. 170; also referred to under the name of Temple of the Sun. A fine example of the order. The column capital is from the design of Pugin, based upon a surviving fragment of the pilaster.

Plate 49. CORINTHIAN. ROMAN. Arch of Constantine, Rome, A.D. 312. A very late example. The moulds above the modillions are too small. As with most triumphal arches, there is both a pedestal and an attic. (See Plate 64 for impost and archivolt.)

Plate 50. CORINTHIAN. ROMAN. Two capitals and other details: (a) Mars Ultor, Rome, 2 B.C.; (b) " Basilica of Antoninus ", Rome.

Plate 51. CORINTHIAN. RENAISSANCE. The order according to Palladio. It excellently represents the normal Roman type.

Plate 52. CORINTHIAN. RENAISSANCE. The order according to Scamozzi. The dentils are omitted from the cornice. (See Plate 54 for his details of the impost and archivolt.)

Plate 53. CORINTHIAN. RENAISSANCE. The order according to Vignola. An excellently proportioned rendering.

Plate 54. CORINTHIAN. RENAISSANCE. The order according to Serlio and Alberti. Alberti's version suffers from the lack of a corona over the modillions.

Plate 55. COMPOSITE. ROMAN. Arch of Titus, Rome, A.D. 82. The earliest instance, in Rome, of the use of the order, which here can only be distinguished from the Corinthian by its capital. The column is engaged and there is both a pedestal and an attic.

Plate 56. COMPOSITE. ROMAN. Arch of Septimius Severus, A.D. 203. The order has both a pedestal and an attic. There are no modillions in the cornice, only dentils. The proportions of the entablature are coarse. (See 64 for attic, impost and archivolt.)

Plate 57. COMPOSITE. ROMAN. From the Central Hall of the Thermae of Diocletian, Rome, A.D. 306. The entablature is indistinguishable from normal Corinthian. A very ornate example.

Plate 58. COMPOSITE. RENAISSANCE. The order according to Palladio. Based, apparently, on the Temple of

Serapis for the entablature. (See Plate 48.)

Plate 59. COMPOSITE. RENAISSANCE. The order according to Scamozzi. He introduces an uncut dentil band into the cornice. (Details of the impost and archivolt are given on Plate 54.)

Plate 60. COMPOSITE. RENAISSANCE. The order according to Vignola. He imparts an Ionic character to the entablature by omitting the block modillions and emphasising the dentils. The acanthus leaves of the capital project too far.

Plate 61. IONIC. GREEK. " Temple of Pandrosus." (The Caryatid Porch of the Erechtheum, Athens, c. 421 B.C.) Six female figures standing upon a pedestal and supporting an entablature of the Ionic early Asiatic type which has cornice and architrave but no frieze.

Plate 62. RENAISSANCE. FRENCH. Caryatides carrying an entablature. An executed work decorating the *Salle des Caryatides*, at the Louvre; by Jean Goujon (d. between 1564 and 1568). The Athenian porch is obviously the inspiration.

Plate 63. ROMAN ENTABLATURES. (a) The Pantheon, including: Entablature of one of the Altars decorating the interior; the second cornice from the ground decorating the exterior of the rotunda; the pilastered order of the second internal tier (these pilasters were removed during the late Italian Renaissance); the entablature crowning the great entrance door externally. The architrave of the latter turns down and frames the door opening (see Plate 67); the entablature crowning the same door internally. (b) Temple of Peace (?), Rome.

Plate 64. ROMAN DETAILS. Various entablatures, imposts and archivolts. Ionic entablature of the second tier and Corinthian entablature of the third tier of the Colosseum, Rome, c. A.D. 75-82; attic and details of imposts and archivolts for large and small arches of the Arch of Septimius Severus, Rome, A.D. 204. (See Plate 56.) Details of imposts and archivolts for large and small arches of the Arch of Constantine, Rome, A.D. 312. (See Plate 49.)

Plate 65. RULES. (a) For establishing a height of entablature in proportion to the height of the order employed; (b) for determining the height of pediments; (c) for the diminution of columns; (d) for the determination of " entasis ".

Plate 66. GREEK DOORWAY. Within the North Porch of the Erechtheum, Athens, c. 421 B.C. (with Roman restorations). The finest and most elaborate Greek instance surviving.

Plate 67. ANTIQUE DOORS AND WINDOWS. (a) Window of the Erechtheum (*Minerva Polias*); (b) window of the Temple of Vesta, Tivoli, c. 80 B.C.; door of the Temple of Vesta, Tivoli. Also, door of the Pantheon, Rome. (See Plate 63.)

Plate 68. RENAISSANCE DOORS. According to designs executed by Vignola: (a) S. Lorenzo, Rome; (b) Farnese Palace, Rome.

Plate 69. RENAISSANCE ARCADES. Three versions of this light and gracious type of arcade, respectively from Ferrara, Rome and Florence, in which arches spring from the caps of columns. The instance from Ferrara shows a rather clumsy angle treatment, typical of Northern Italy, in which a small pilaster joins the angle column with the entablature. The example from Rome is much more satisfactory in this regard. The third example shows an angle treatment in an internal court.

Plate 70. GREEK TEMPLE DESIGN. Plan and elevation of the Parthenon, 447 B.C., illustrating the principal features normal to Greek Doric temples. The lower drawings show the small temple of Niké Apteros, 438 B.C., also on the acropolis at Athens, an equally fine instance of the Ionic order.

Plate 71. ROMAN DETAILS. A series of details of decorative panels occurring on the underside of architraves of various Roman monuments.

Plate 72. ORNAMENTAL DETAILS OF MOULDINGS (Roman).

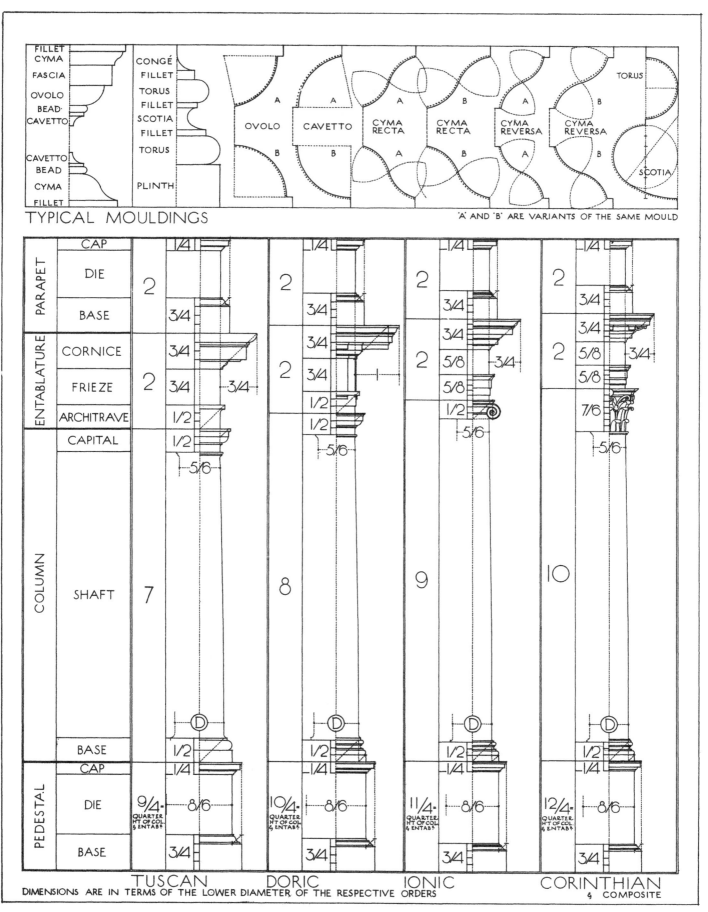

TYPICAL MOULDINGS

'A' AND 'B' ARE VARIANTS OF THE SAME MOULD

A METHOD OF DRAWING THE RENAISSANCE ORDERS. Proportions expressed in terms of the lower diameter (D) of the column. *Above: Typical Renaissance mouldings. Below: Principal proportions*

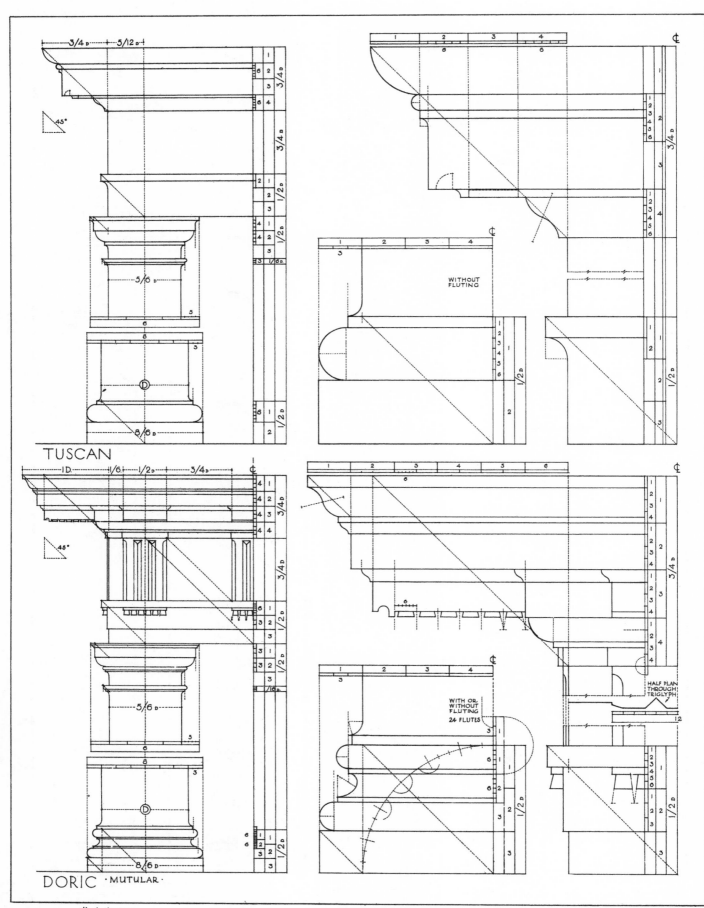

TUSCAN

DORIC ·MUTULAR·

R. A. Cordingley

B. METHOD OF DRAWING THE RENAISSANCE ORDERS. Proportions of the column and entablature of the orders expressed in terms of the lower diameter (D) of the column. *Above: The Tuscan order. Below: The Doric (Mutular) order.*

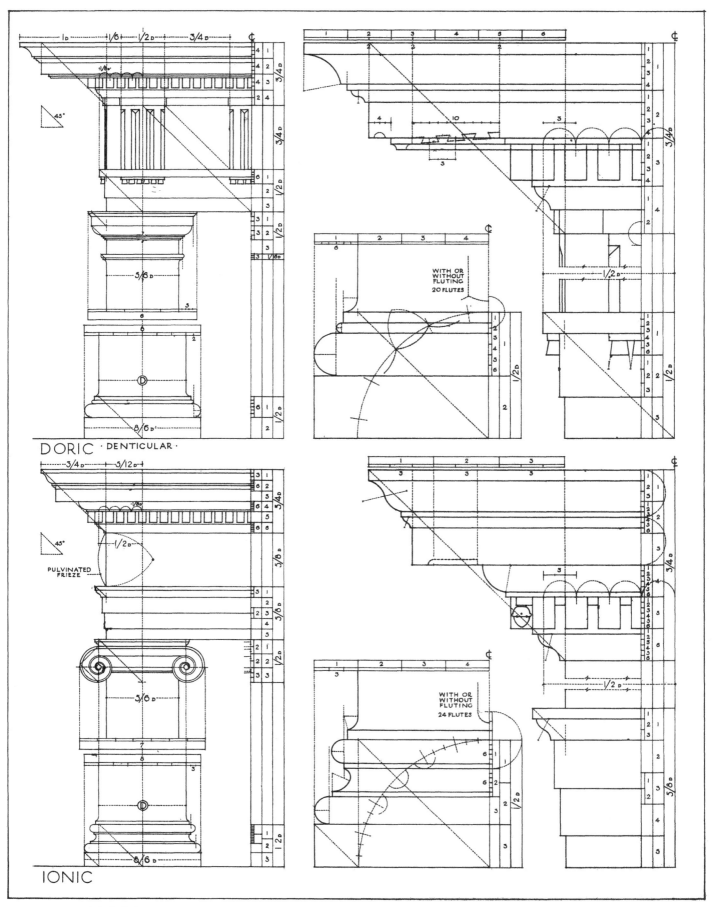

DORIC ·DENTICULAR·

IONIC

WITH OR WITHOUT FLUTING 20 FLUTES

WITH OR WITHOUT FLUTING 24 FLUTES

PULVINATED FRIEZE

R. A. Cordingley

C METHOD OF DRAWING THE RENAISSANCE ORDERS. Proportions of the column and entablature of the orders, expressed in terms of the lower diameter (D) of the column. *Above: The Doric (Denticular) order. Below: The Ionic order.*

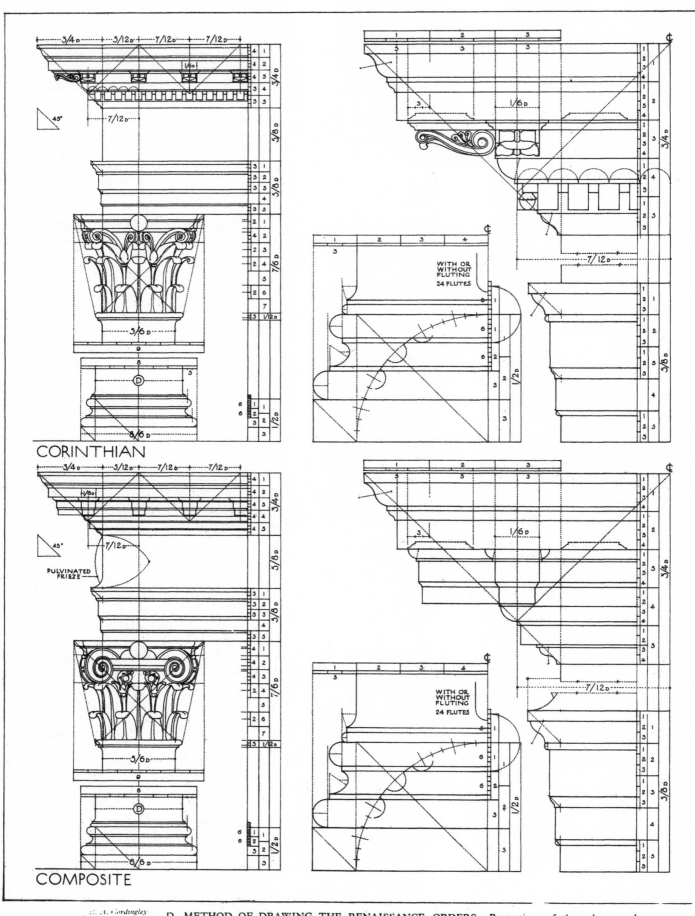

CORINTHIAN

COMPOSITE

D METHOD OF DRAWING THE RENAISSANCE ORDERS. Proportions of the column and entablature of the orders, expressed in terms of the lower diameter (D) of the column. *Above: The Corinthian order. Below: The Composite order.*

E   TYPES of colonnade and arcade.

R. A. Cordingley

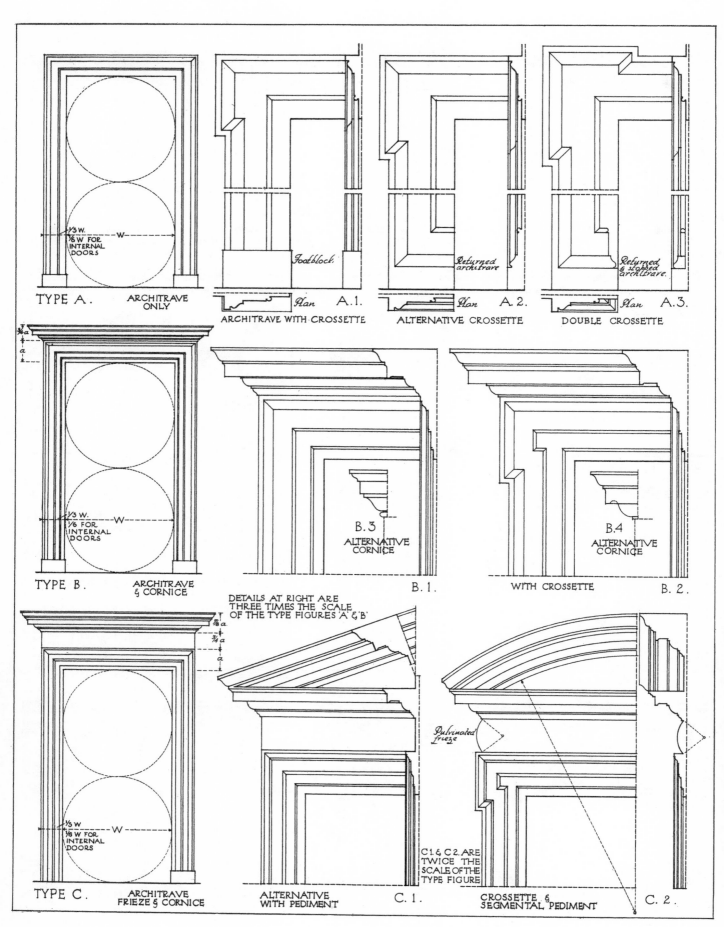

TYPE A.   ARCHITRAVE ONLY

¹⁄₃ W.
¹⁄₆ W FOR
INTERNAL
DOORS
W

Footblock.
Plan   A.1.
ARCHITRAVE WITH CROSSETTE

Returned architrave
Plan   A.2.
ALTERNATIVE CROSSETTE

Returned & stopped architrave.
Plan   A.3.
DOUBLE CROSSETTE

TYPE B.   ARCHITRAVE & CORNICE

¹⁄₃ W.
¹⁄₆ FOR
INTERNAL
DOORS
W

B.3
ALTERNATIVE CORNICE

B.1.

B.4
ALTERNATIVE CORNICE

WITH CROSSETTE   B.2.

TYPE C.   ARCHITRAVE FRIEZE & CORNICE

¹⁄₃ W
¹⁄₆ W FOR
INTERNAL
DOORS
W

DETAILS AT RIGHT ARE
THREE TIMES THE SCALE
OF THE TYPE FIGURES 'A' & 'B'

ALTERNATIVE
WITH PEDIMENT   C.1.

C1. & C2. ARE
TWICE THE
SCALE OF THE
TYPE FIGURE

Pulvinated frieze

CROSSETTE &
SEGMENTAL PEDIMENT   C.2.

R. A. Cordingley

F   DOOR OPENINGS, simple types.

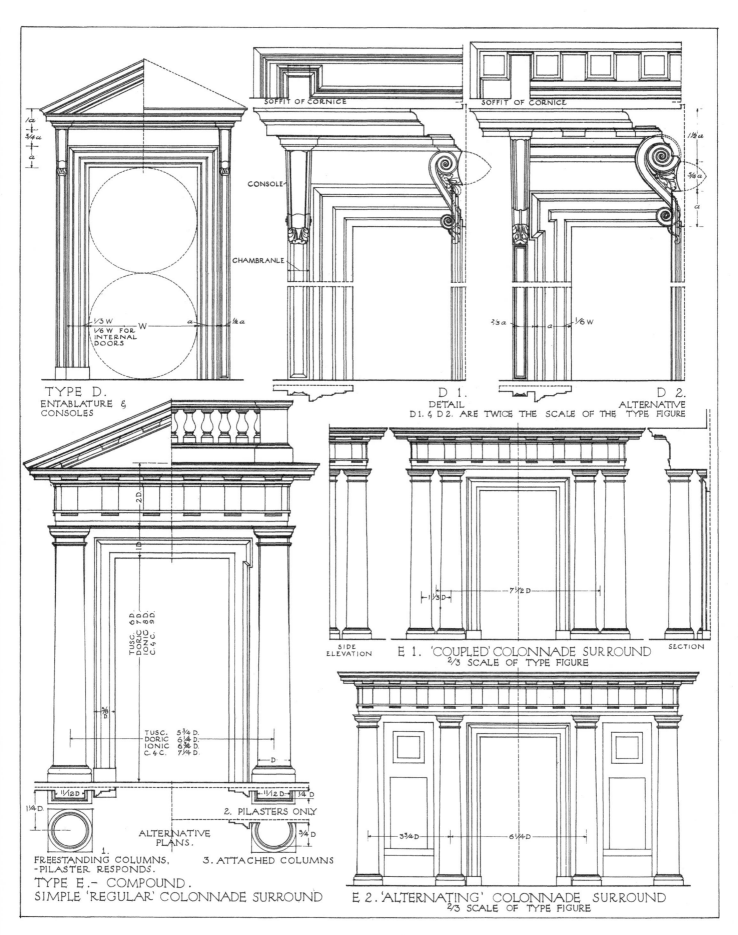

TYPE D.
ENTABLATURE &
CONSOLES

1/3 W
1/6 W FOR
INTERNAL
DOORS

CONSOLE

CHAMBRANLE

SOFFIT OF CORNICE

SOFFIT OF CORNICE

D 1.
DETAIL

D 2.
ALTERNATIVE

D 1. & D 2. ARE TWICE THE SCALE OF THE TYPE FIGURE

TUSC. 6 D.
DORIC 7 D.
IONIC 8 D.
C. & C. 9 D.

TUSC. 5 3/4 D.
DORIC 6 1/4 D.
IONIC 6 3/4 D.
C. & C. 7 1/4 D.

SIDE
ELEVATION

E 1. 'COUPLED' COLONNADE SURROUND
2/3 SCALE OF TYPE FIGURE

SECTION

ALTERNATIVE
PLANS.

1.
FREESTANDING COLUMNS,
-PILASTER RESPONDS.

2. PILASTERS ONLY

3. ATTACHED COLUMNS

TYPE E.- COMPOUND.
SIMPLE 'REGULAR' COLONNADE SURROUND

E 2. 'ALTERNATING' COLONNADE SURROUND
2/3 SCALE OF TYPE FIGURE

G DOOR OPENINGS, double and compound types.

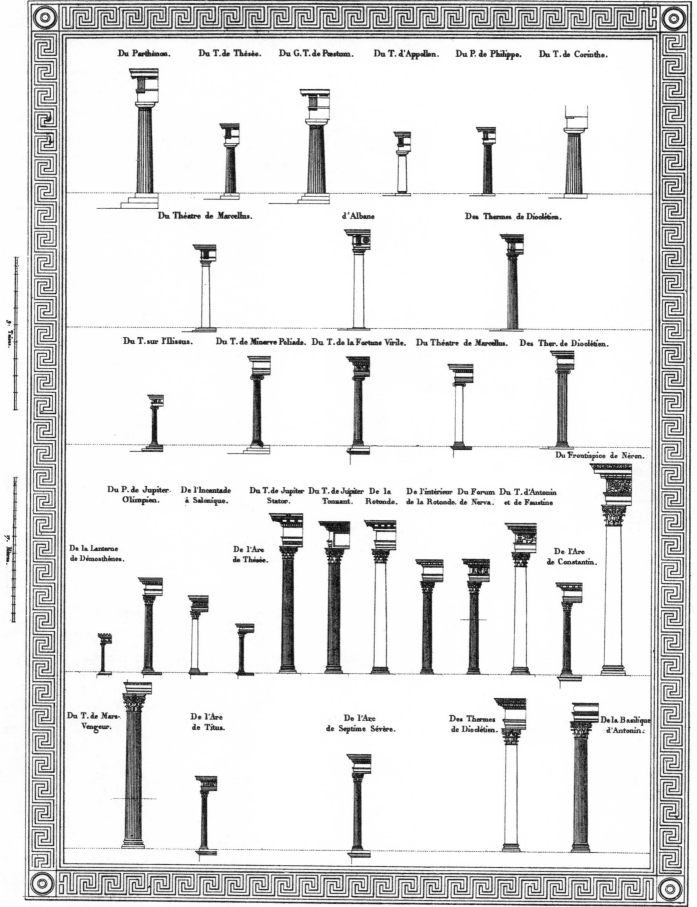

Du Parthénon.   Du T. de Thésée.   Du G. T. de Pœstum.   Du T. d'Appollon.   Du P. de Philippe.   Du T. de Corinthe.

Du Théatre de Marcellus.   d'Albane   Des Thermes de Dioclétien.

Du T. sur l'Ilissus.   Du T. de Minerve Poliade.   Du T. de la Fortune Virile.   Du Théatre de Marcellus.   Des Ther. de Dioclétien.

Du Frontispice de Néron.

Du P. de Jupiter Olimpien.   De l'Incantade à Salonique.   Du T. de Jupiter Stator.   Du T. de Jupiter Tonnant.   De la Rotonde.   De l'intérieur de la Rotonde.   Du Forum de Nerva.   Du T. d'Antonin et de Faustine

De la Lanterne de Démosthènes.   De l'Arc de Thésée.   De l'Arc de Constantin.

Du T. de Mars-Vengeur.   De l'Arc de Titus.   De l'Arc de Septime Sévère.   Des Thermes de Dioclétien.   De la Basilique d'Antonin.

Normand frontispiece   (FRONTISPIECE.) PARALLEL OF ANTIQUE ORDERS, included among the original plates following, showing their relative actual dimensions.

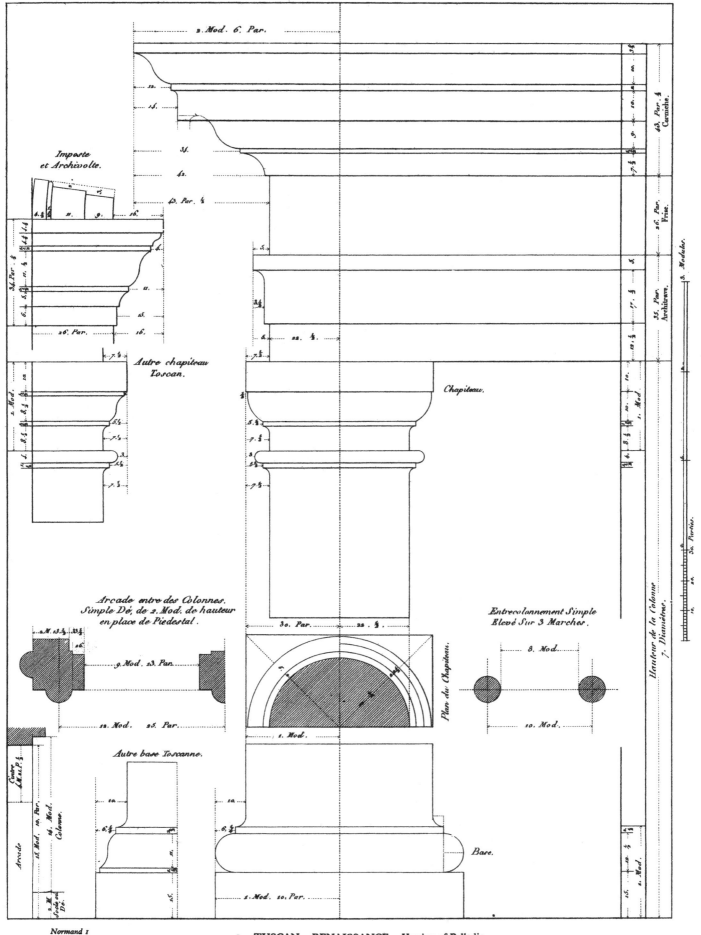

Imposte
et Archivolte.

Autre chapiteau
Toscan.

Chapiteau.

Arcade entre des Colonnes.
Simple Dé, de 2. Mod. de hauteur
en place de Piedestal.

Entrecolonnement Simple
Elevé Sur 3 Marches.

Plan du Chapiteau.

Autre base Toscanne.

Base.

Arcade

Hauteur de la Colonne
7. Diamètres.

Corniche.
Frise.
Architrave.

2. Mod. 6. Par.

30. Par.   22. ¼.

8. Mod.

10. Mod.

1. Mod.

1. Mod. 10. Par.

9. Mod. 13. Par.

12. Mod. 23. Par.

1. TUSCAN. RENAISSANCE. Version of Palladio.

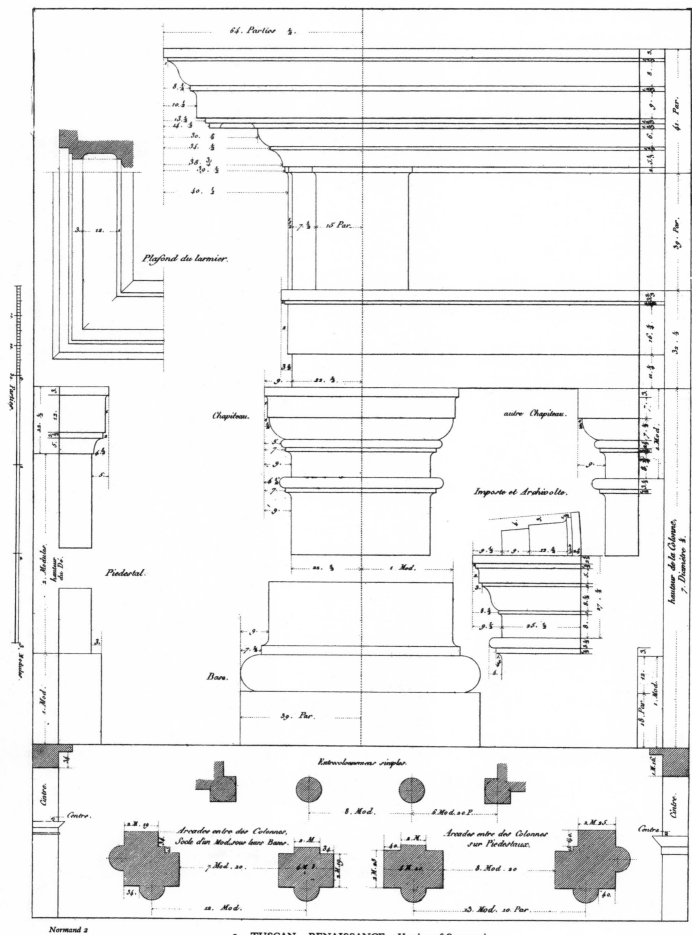

64. Parties ½.

Plafond du larmier.

15. Par.

Chapiteau.

autre Chapiteau.

Imposte et Archivolte.

Piedestal.

Base.

39. Par.

hauteur de la Colonne,
7. Diamètre ⅓.

Entrecolonnemens simples.

8. Mod.   6. Mod. 20 P.

Arcades entre des Colonnes,
Socle d'un Mod. sous leurs Bases.

7. Mod. 20.

12. Mod.

Arcades entre des Colonnes
sur Piedestaux.

8. Mod. 20.

13. Mod. 10. Par.

Centre.   Centre.   Centre.

2. TUSCAN.   RENAISSANCE.   Version of Scamozzi.

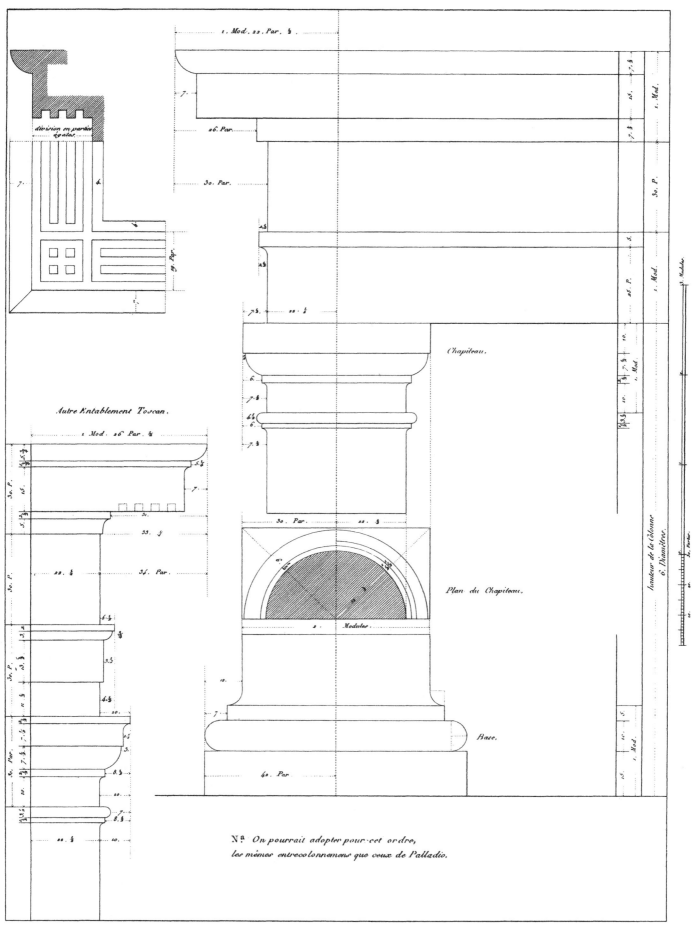

division en parties égales.

Autre Entablement Toscan.

Chapiteau.

Plan du Chapiteau.

Base.

Nᵃ On pourrait adopter pour cet ordre,
les mêmes entrecolonnemens que ceux de Palladio.

hauteur de la Colonne
6. Diamètres.

3. TUSCAN. RENAISSANCE. Version of Serlio.

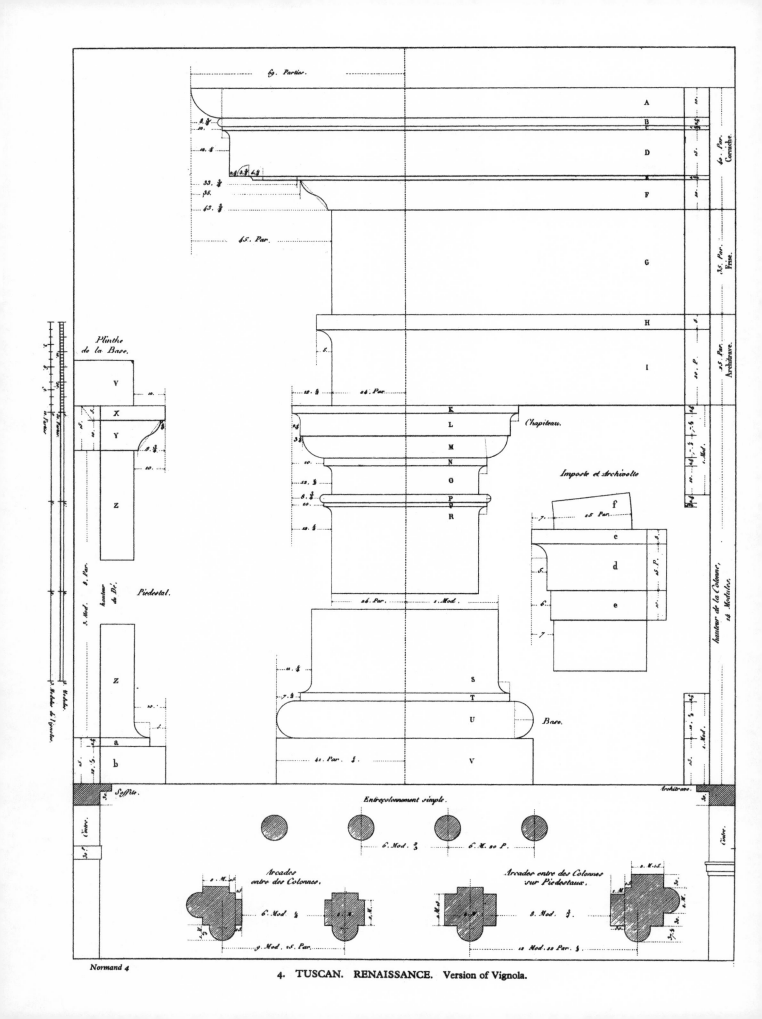

4. TUSCAN. RENAISSANCE. Version of Vignola.

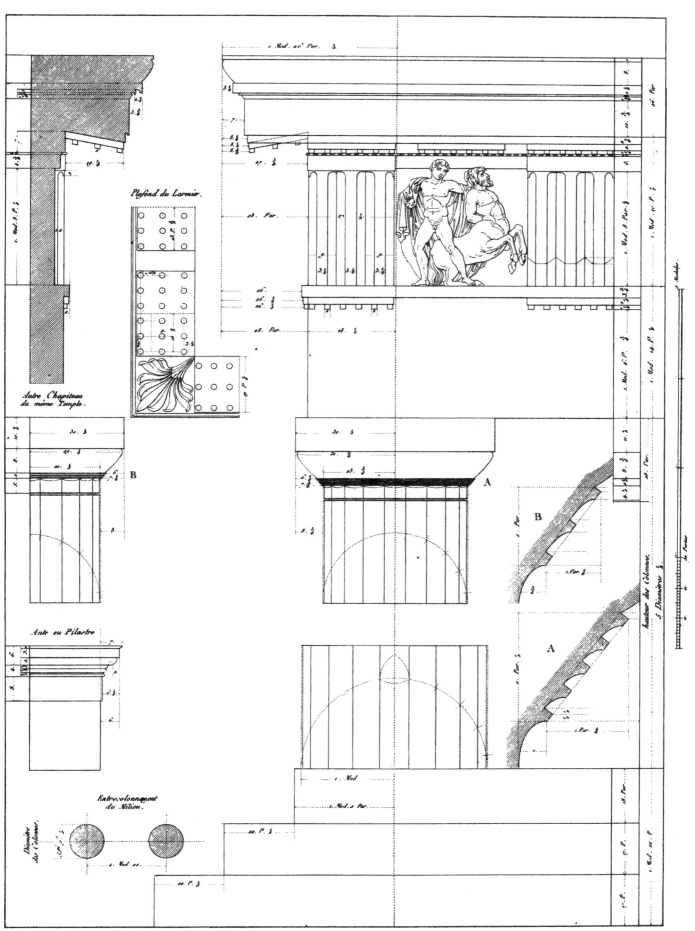

Plafond du Larmier.

Autre Chapiteau
du même Temple.

Ante ou Pilastre

Entrecolonnement
du Milieu.

Diamètre
des Colonnes.

hauteur des Colonnes.
5 Diamètres ½.

5. DORIC. GREEK. The Parthenon, Athens.

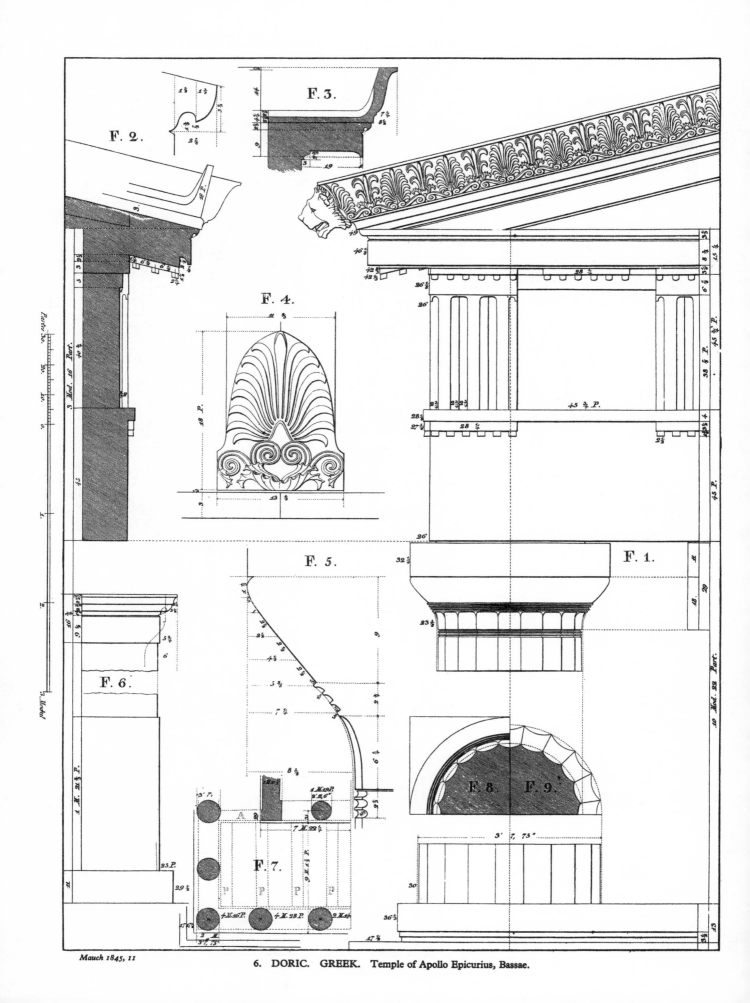

F. 2.

F. 3.

F. 4.

F. 5.

F. 6.

F. 7.

F. 1.

F. 8.   F. 9.

6. DORIC. GREEK. Temple of Apollo Epicurius, Bassae.

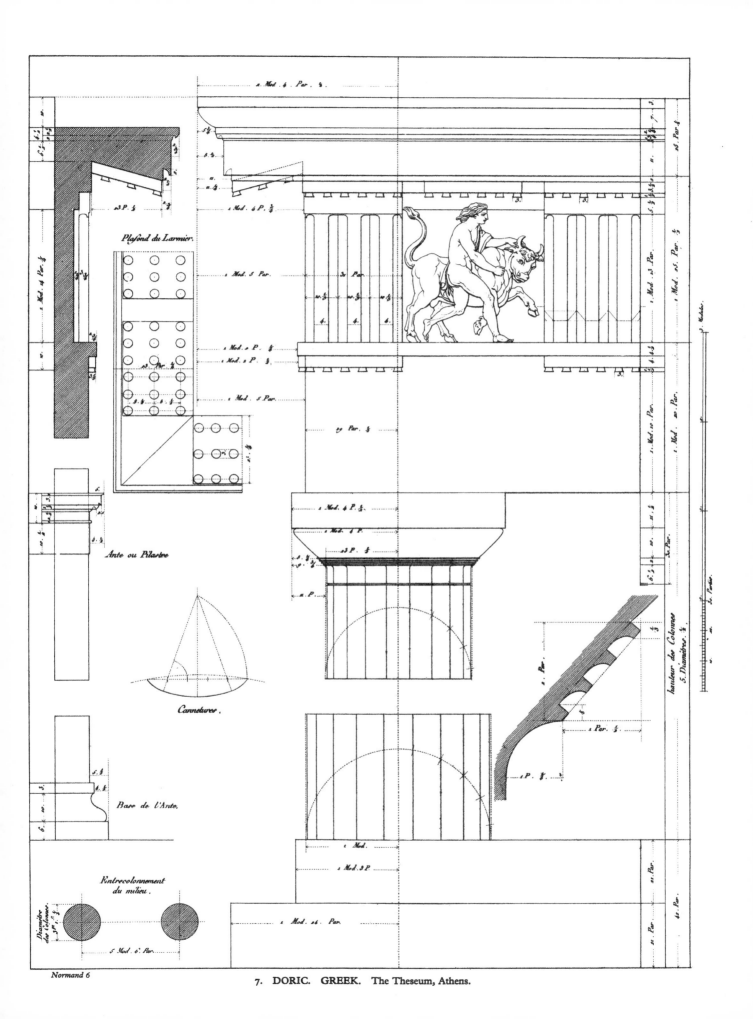

7. DORIC. GREEK. The Theseum, Athens.

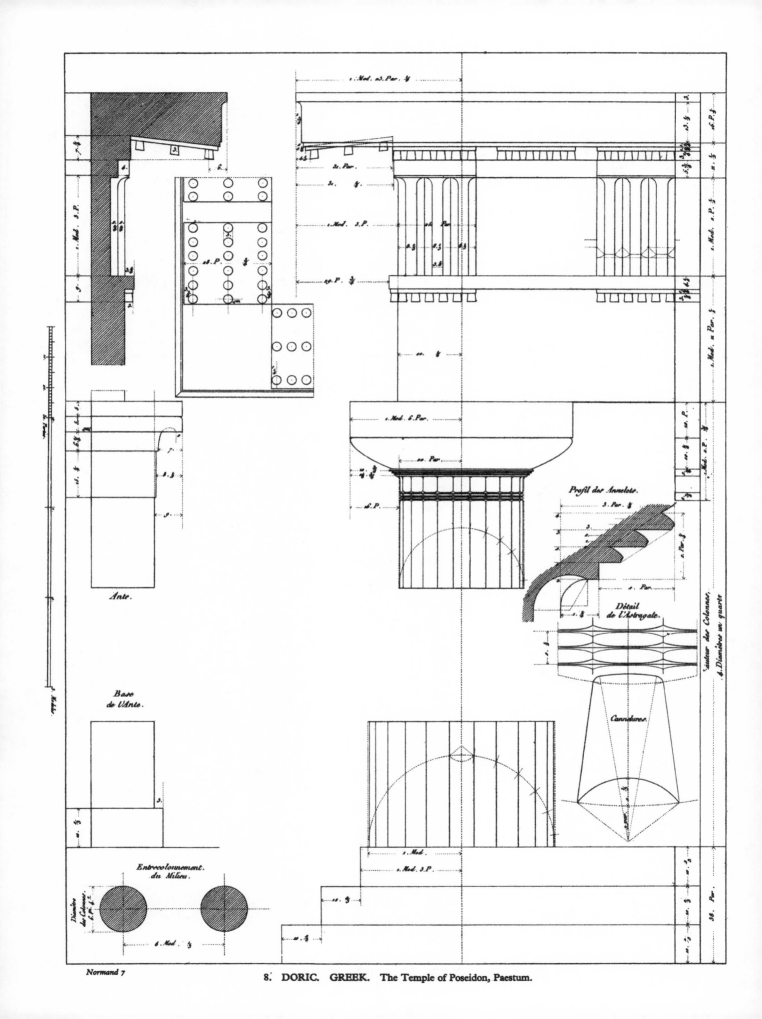

Ante.

Base
de l'Ante.

Entrecolonnement.
du Milieu.

Profil des Annelets.

Détail
de l'Astragale.

Cannelures.

8. DORIC. GREEK. The Temple of Poseidon, Paestum.

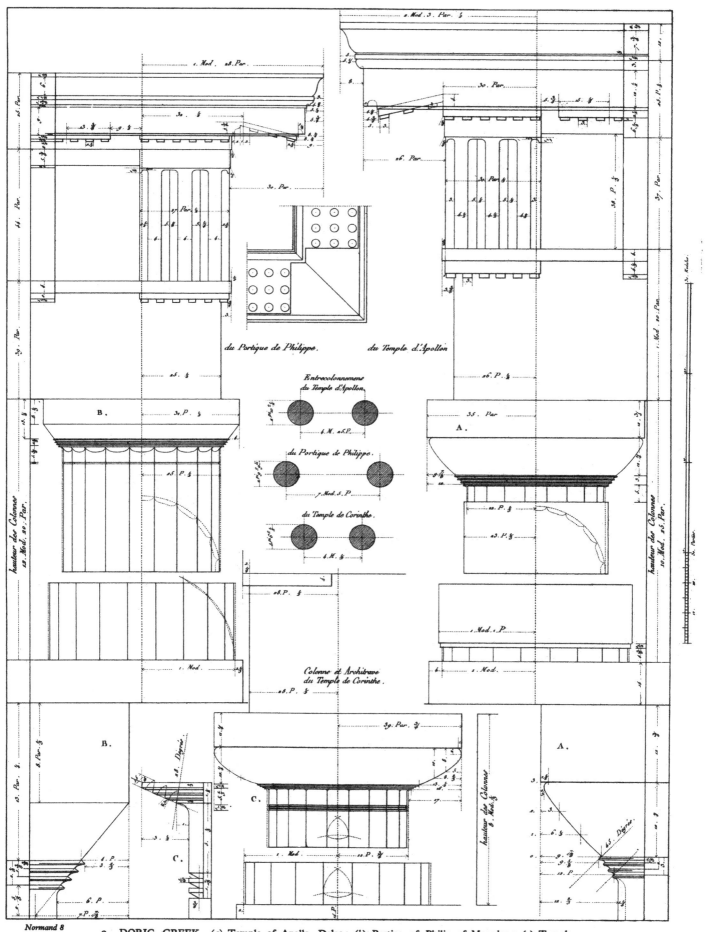

9. DORIC. GREEK. (*a*) Temple of Apollo, Delos; (*b*) Portico of Philip of Macedon; (*c*) Temple of Apollo, Corinth.

du Portique de Philippe.

du Temple d'Apollon

Entrecolonnemens
du Temple d'Apollon

du Portique de Philippe.

du Temple de Corinthe.

Colonne et Architrave
du Temple de Corinthe.

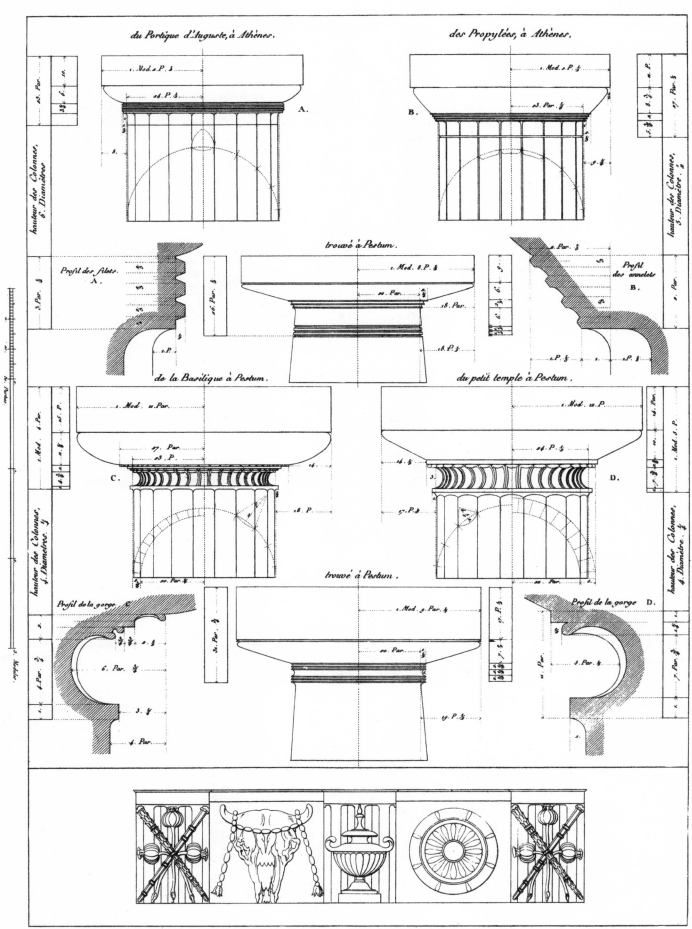

du Portique d'Auguste, à Athènes.

des Propylées, à Athènes.

trouvé à Pestum.

de la Basilique à Pestum.

du petit temple à Pestum.

trouvé à Pestum.

10. DORIC. GREEK. Various Capitals. (See Index.)

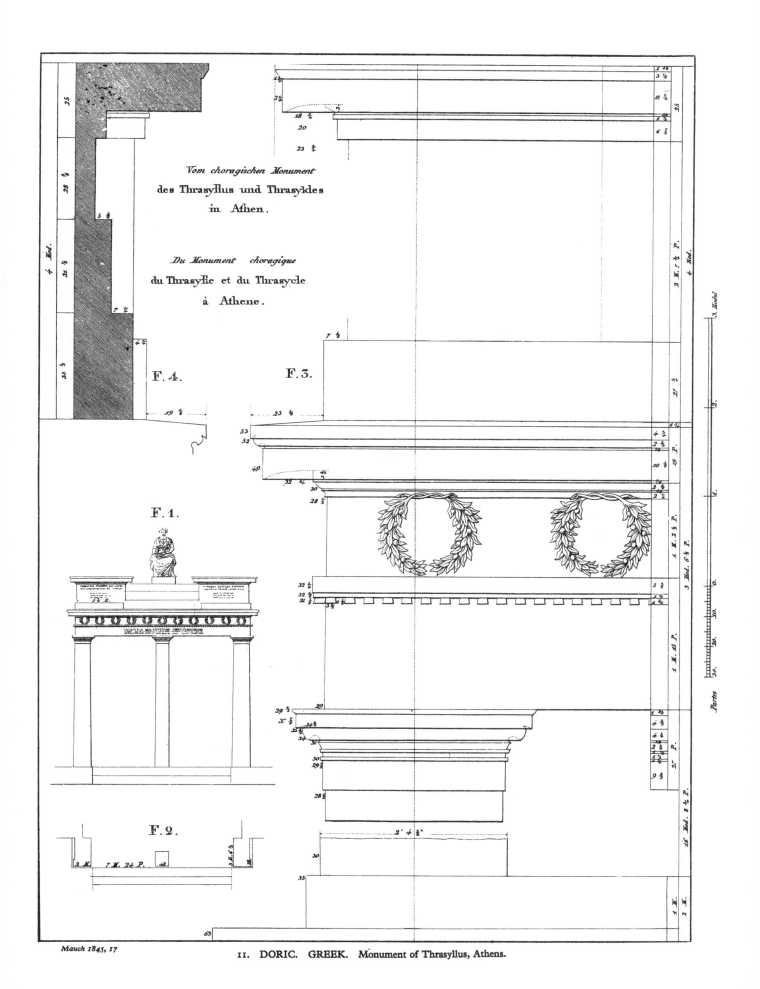

Vom choragischen Monument
des Thrasyllus und Thrasykles
in Athen.

Du Monument choragique
du Thrasylle et du Thrasycle
à Athene.

F. 4.

F. 3.

F. 1.

F. 2.

II. DORIC. GREEK. Monument of Thrasyllus, Athens.

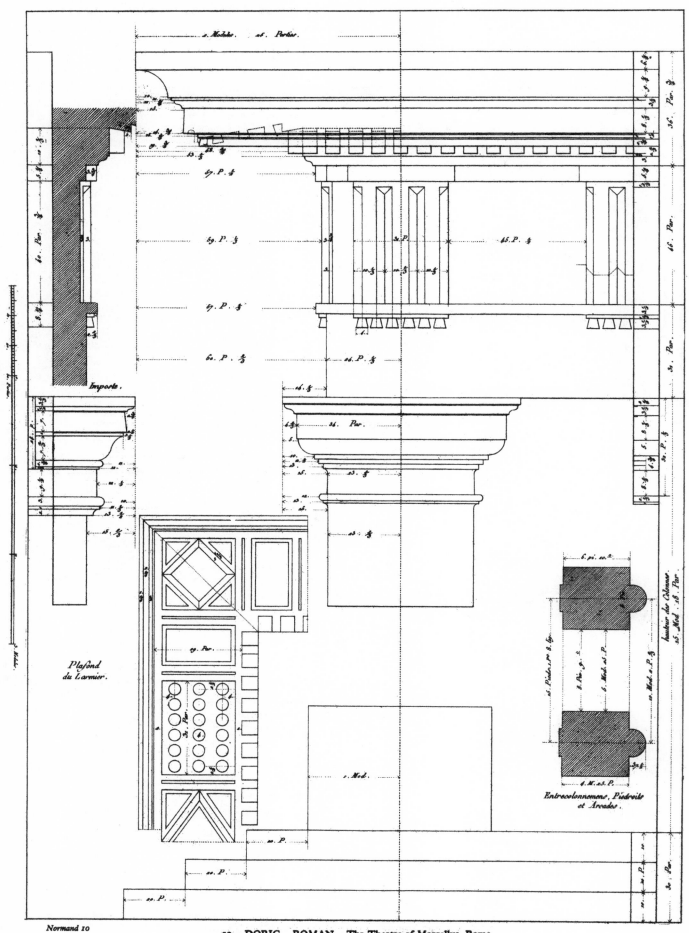

Imposte.

Plafond
du Larmier.

Entrecolonnemens, Piédroits
et Arcades.

12. DORIC. ROMAN. The Theatre of Marcellus, Rome.

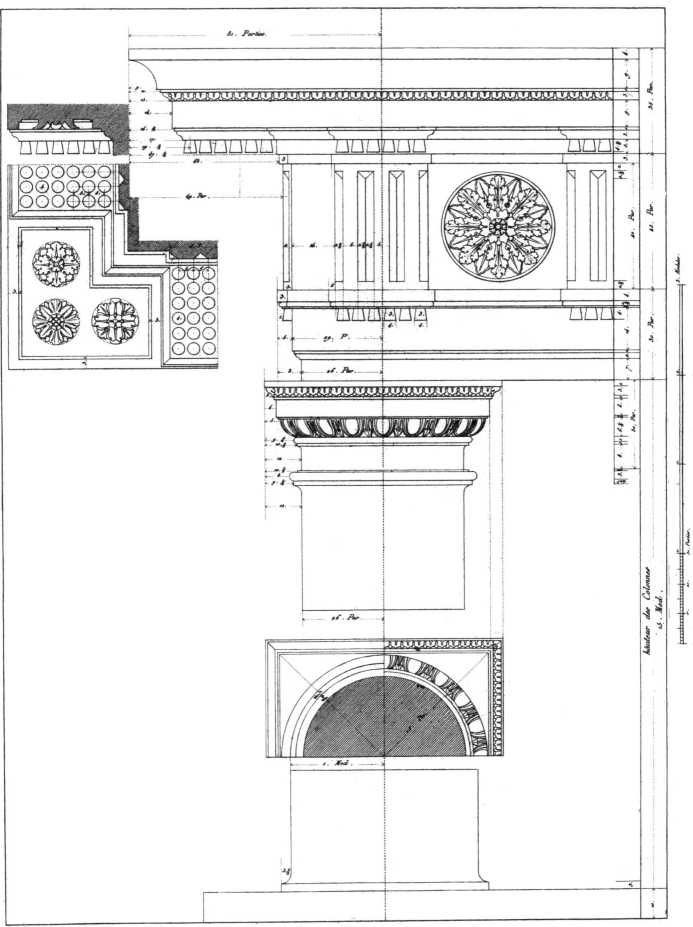

13. DORIC. ROMAN. From a building at Albáno, near Rome.

14. DORIC. ROMAN. Thermae of Diocletian, Rome.

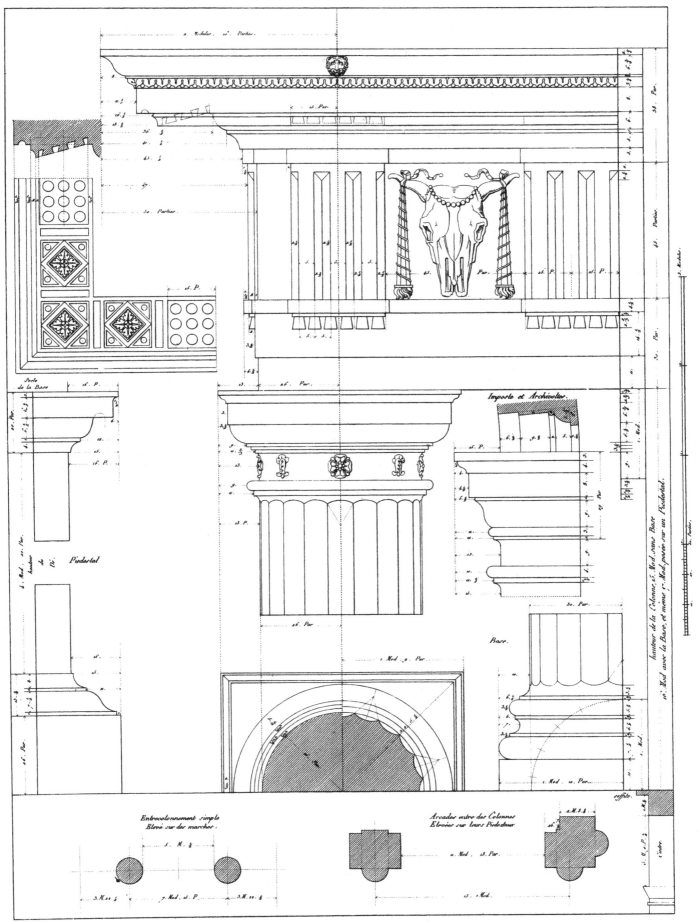

15. DORIC. RENAISSANCE. Version of Palladio.

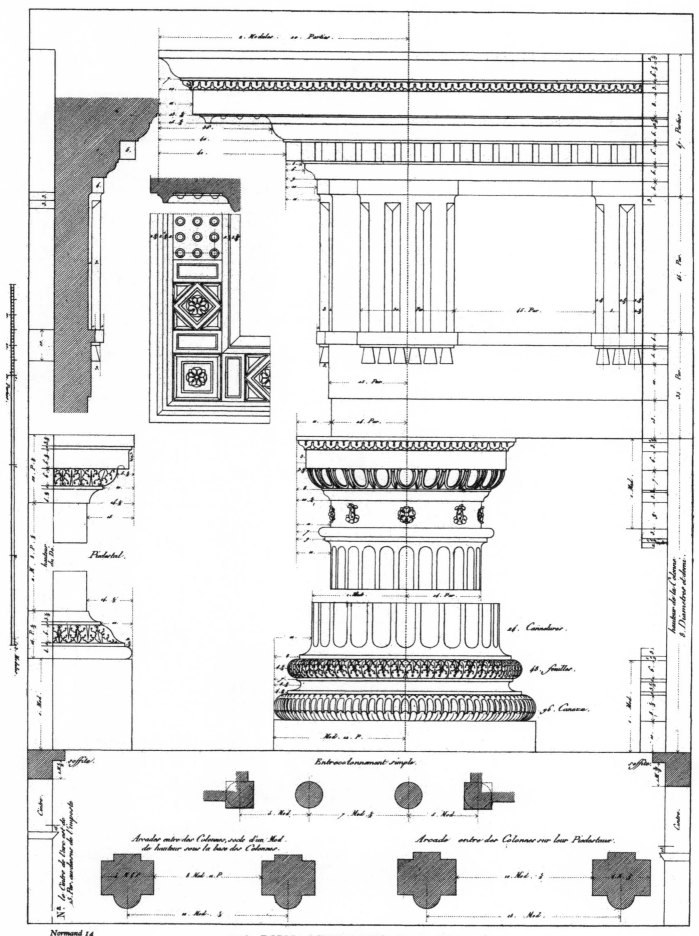

Piedestal.

24. Cannelures.

45. feuilles.

96. Canaux.

Entrecolonnement simple.

Arcades entre des Colonnes, socle d'un Mod.
de hauteur sous la base des Colonnes.

Arcade entre des Colonnes sur leur Piedestaux.

16. DORIC. RENAISSANCE. Version of Scamozzi.

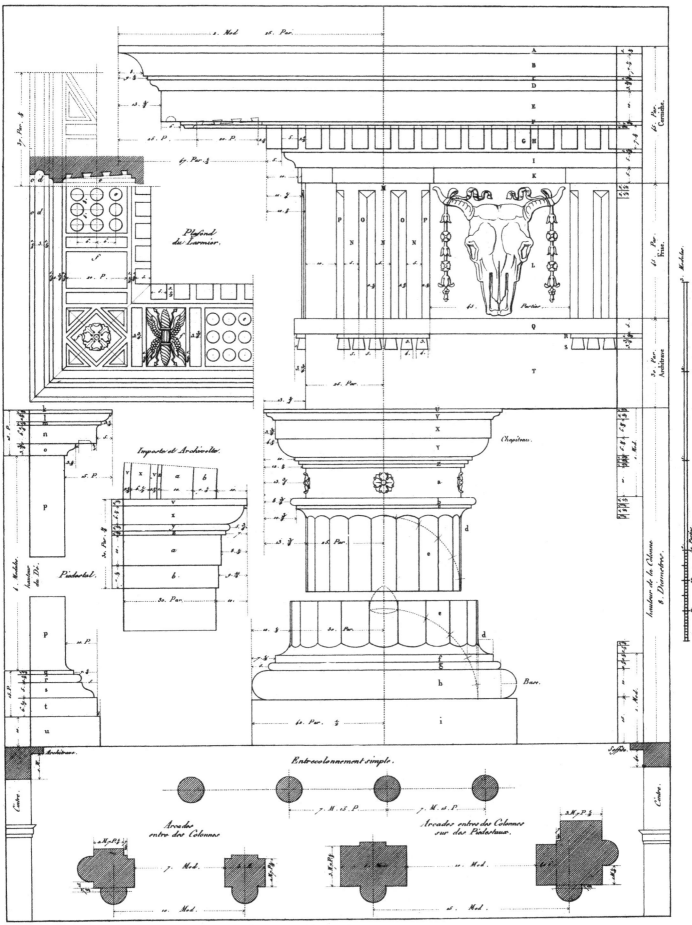

Plafond
du Larmier.

Imposte et Archivolte.

Piédestal.

Chapiteau.

Base.

Entrecolonnement simple.

Arcades
entre des Colonnes

Arcades entres des Colonnes
sur des Piédestaux.

17. DORIC. RENAISSANCE. Denticular version of Vignola.

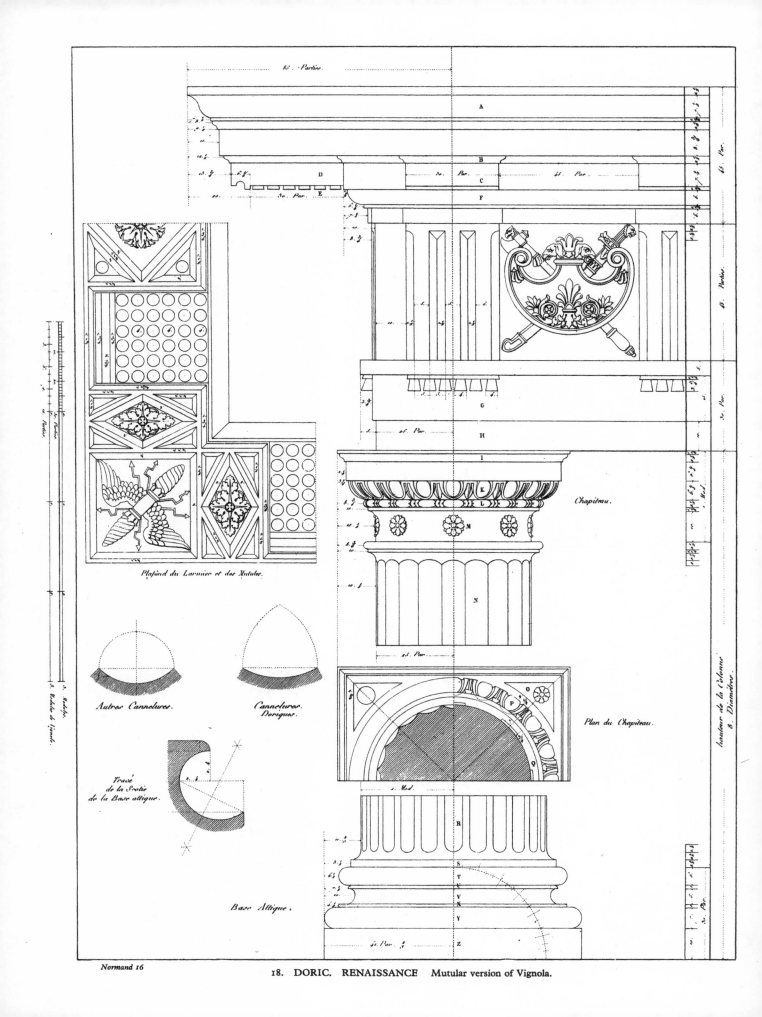

Plafond du Larmier et des Mutules.

Autres Cannelures.

Cannelures Doriques.

Tracé de la Scotie de la Base attique.

Chapiteau.

Plan du Chapiteau.

Base Attique.

Hauteur de la Colonne. 8. Diamètres.

18. DORIC. RENAISSANCE   Mutular version of Vignola.

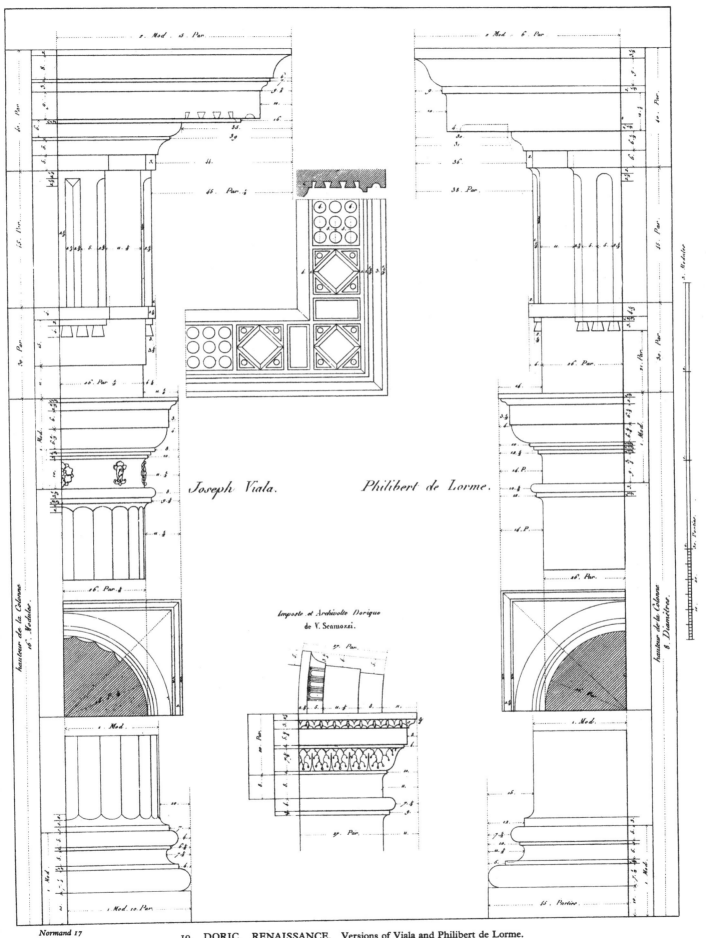

Joseph Viala.   *Philibert de Lorme.*

Imposte et Archivolte Dorique
de V. Scamozzi.

19. DORIC. RENAISSANCE. Versions of Viala and Philibert de Lorme.

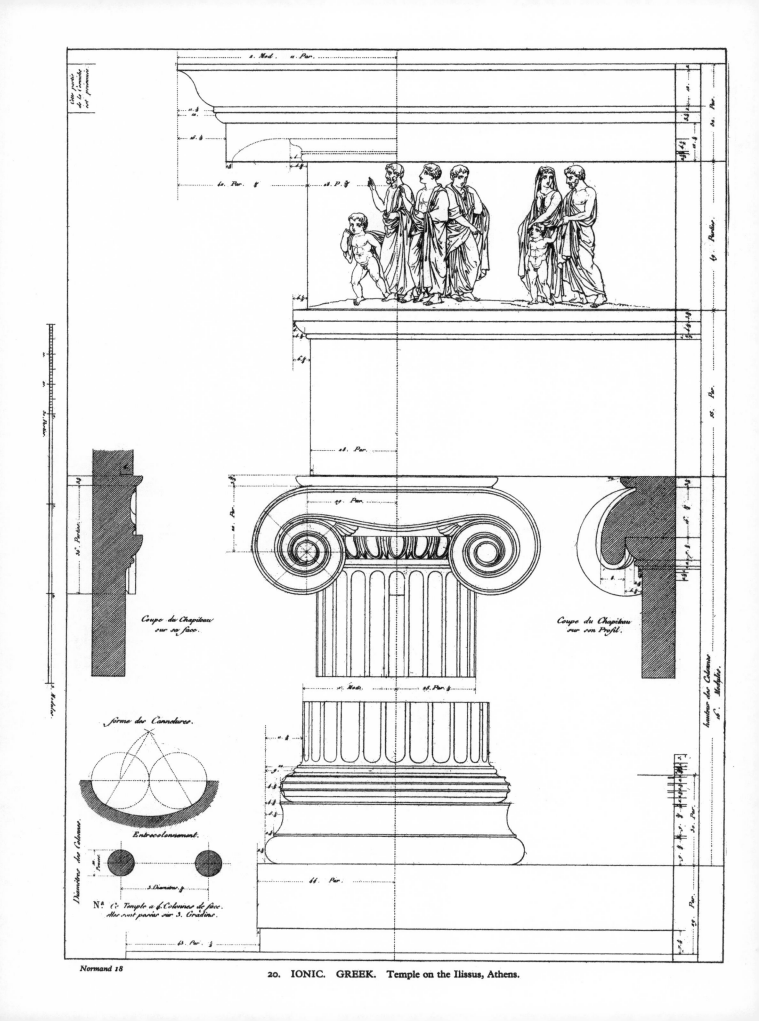

Coupe du Chapiteau
sur sa face.

Coupe du Chapiteau
sur son Profil.

forme des Cannelures.

Entrecolonnement.

Diamètres des Colonnes.

Nᵃ. Ce Temple a 4. Colonnes de face.
elles sont posées sur 3. Gradins.

20. IONIC. GREEK. Temple on the Ilissus, Athens.

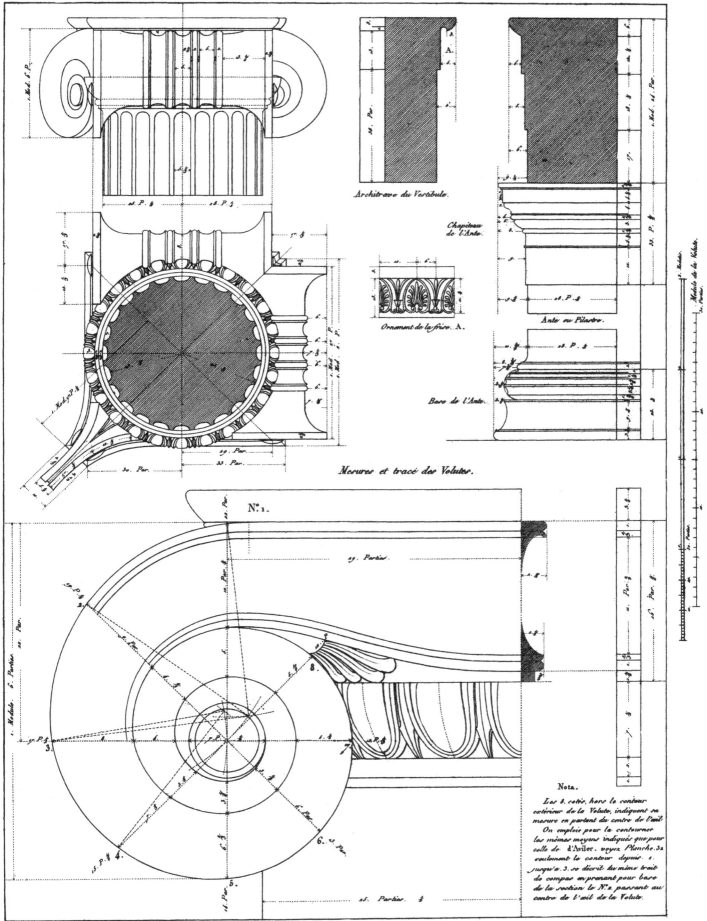

Architrave du Vestibule.

Chapiteau
de l'Ante.

Ornement de la frise. A.

Ante ou Pilastre.

Base de l'Ante.

Mesures et tracé des Volutes.

N.º 1.

Nota.

Les 8 côtés, hors le contour
extérieur de la Volute, indiquent sa
mesure en partant du centre de l'œil.
On emploie pour la contourner
les mêmes moyens indiqués que pour
celle de d'Aviler. voyez Planche 32
seulement le contour depuis 1.
jusqu'à 3. se décrit du même trait
de compas en prenant pour base
de la section le N.º 2 passant au
centre de l'œil de la Volute.

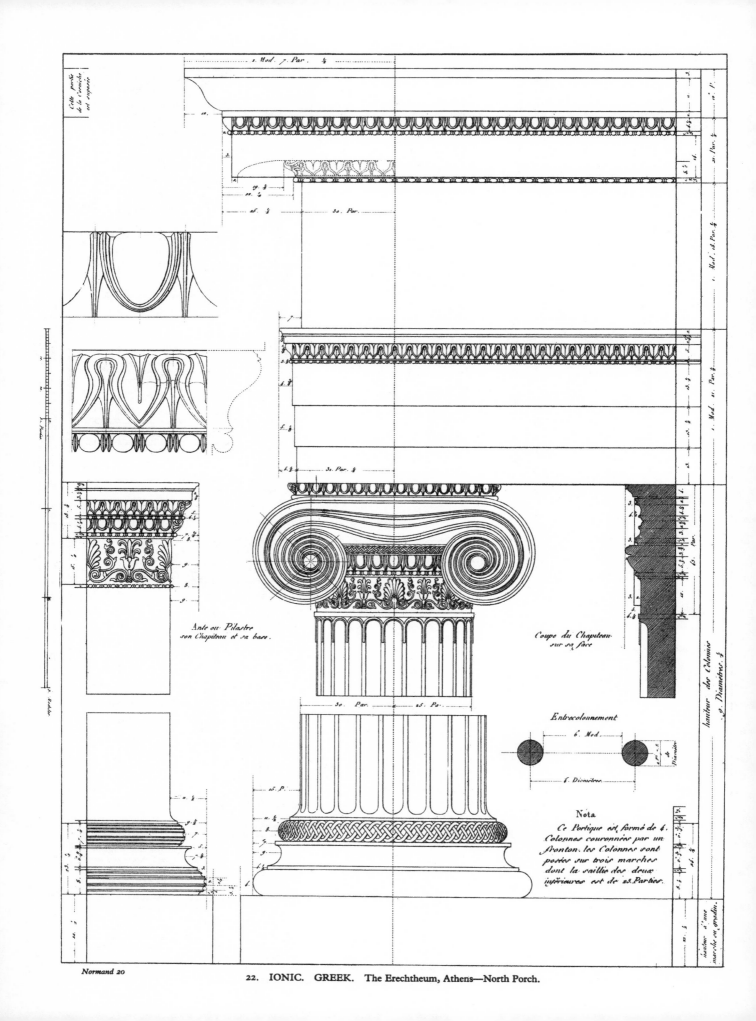

22. IONIC. GREEK. The Erechtheum, Athens—North Porch.

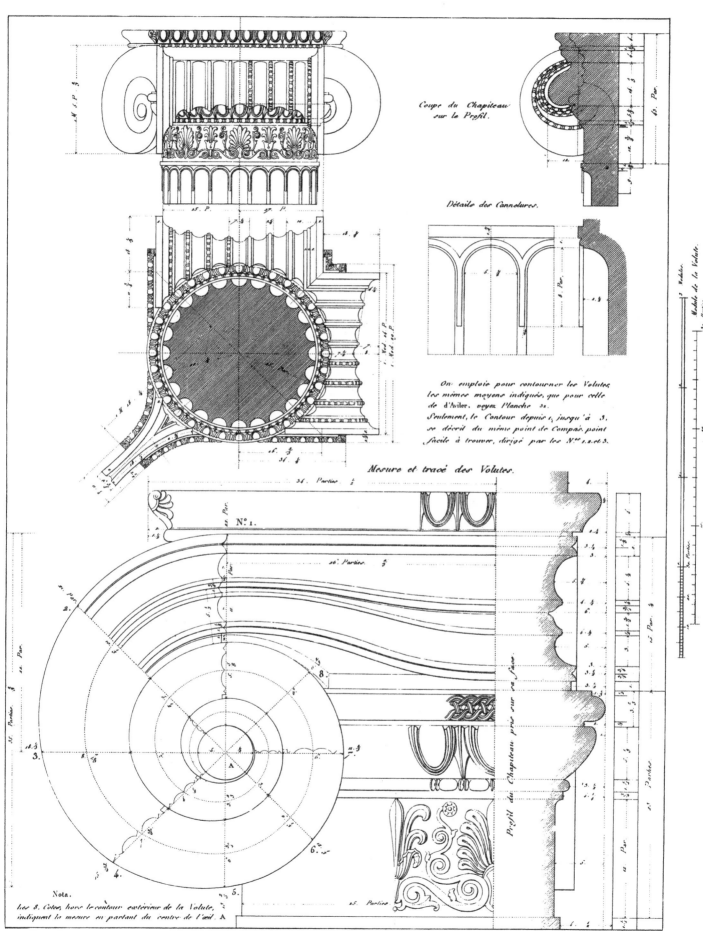

Coupe du Chapiteau
sur le Profil.

Détaile des Cannelures.

On emploie pour contourner les Volutes,
les mêmes moyens indiqués, que pour celle
de d'Aviler. voyez Planche 31.
Seulement, le Contour depuis 1, jusqu'à 3,
se décrit du même point de Compas. point
facile à trouver, dirigé par les N.os 1.2.et 3.

Mesure et tracé des Volutes.

Profil du Chapiteau pris sur sa face.

Module de la Volute.

Nota.
les 8. Cotes, hors le contour extérieur de la Volute,
indiquent la mesure en partant du centre de l'œil. A

23. IONIC. GREEK. The Erechtheum, Athens—details of capital from the North Porch. (*See* Plate 22.)

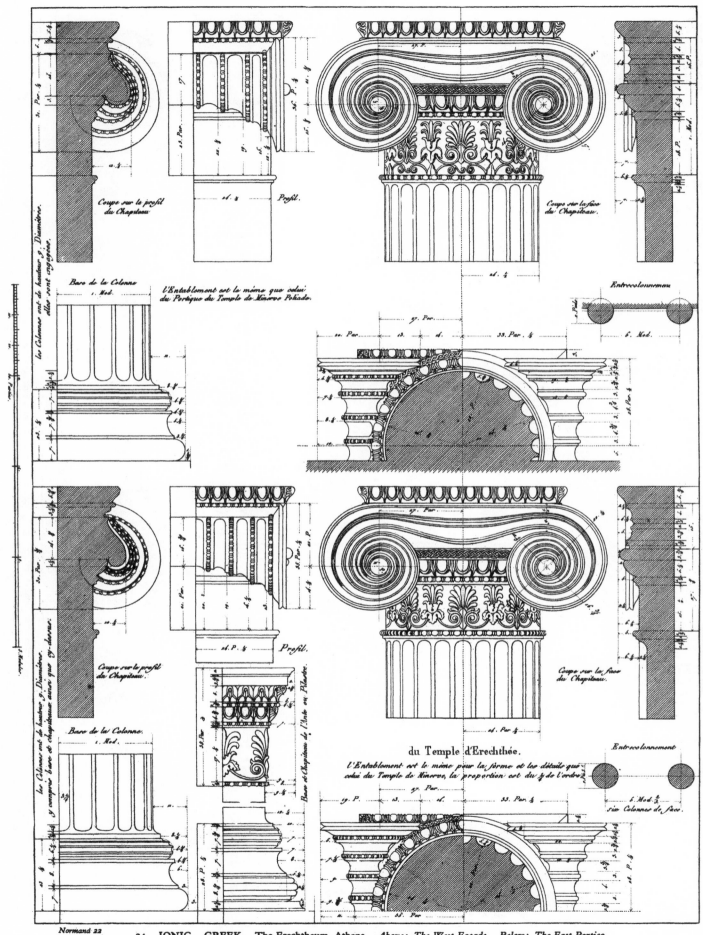

Coupe sur le profil
du Chapiteau.

Profil.

Coupe sur la face
du Chapiteau.

Base de la Colonne.
1. Mod.

L'Entablement est le même que celui
du Portique du Temple de Minerve Poliade.

Entrecolonnement

Coupe sur le profil
du Chapiteau.

Profil.

Coupe sur la face
du Chapiteau.

Base de la Colonne.
1. Mod.

Base et Chapiteau de l'Ante ou Pilastre.

du Temple d'Erechthée.

L'Entablement est le même pour la forme et les détails que
celui du Temple de Minerve, la proportion est du ⅚ de l'ordre.

Entrecolonnement

6. Mod. ⅔
six Colonnes de face.

24. IONIC. GREEK. The Erechtheum, Athens. *Above: The West Facade. Below: The East Portico.*

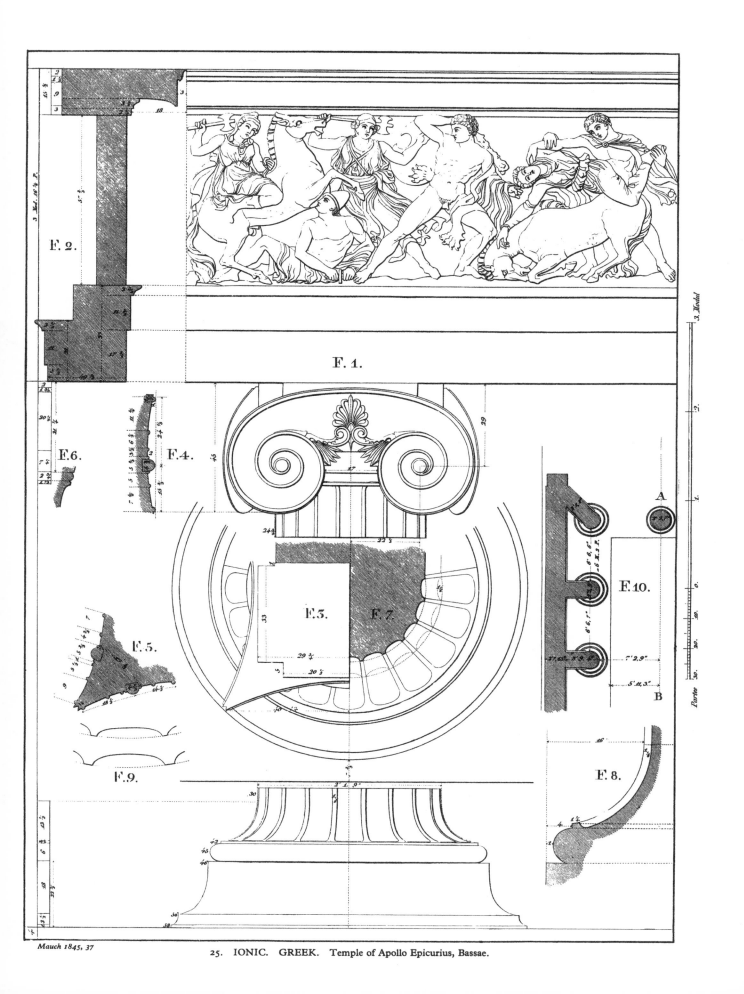

F. 2.

F. 1.

F.6.

F.4.

F.5.

F.3.

F.7.

F.9.

F.8.

A

F.10.

B

25. IONIC. GREEK. Temple of Apollo Epicurius, Bassae.

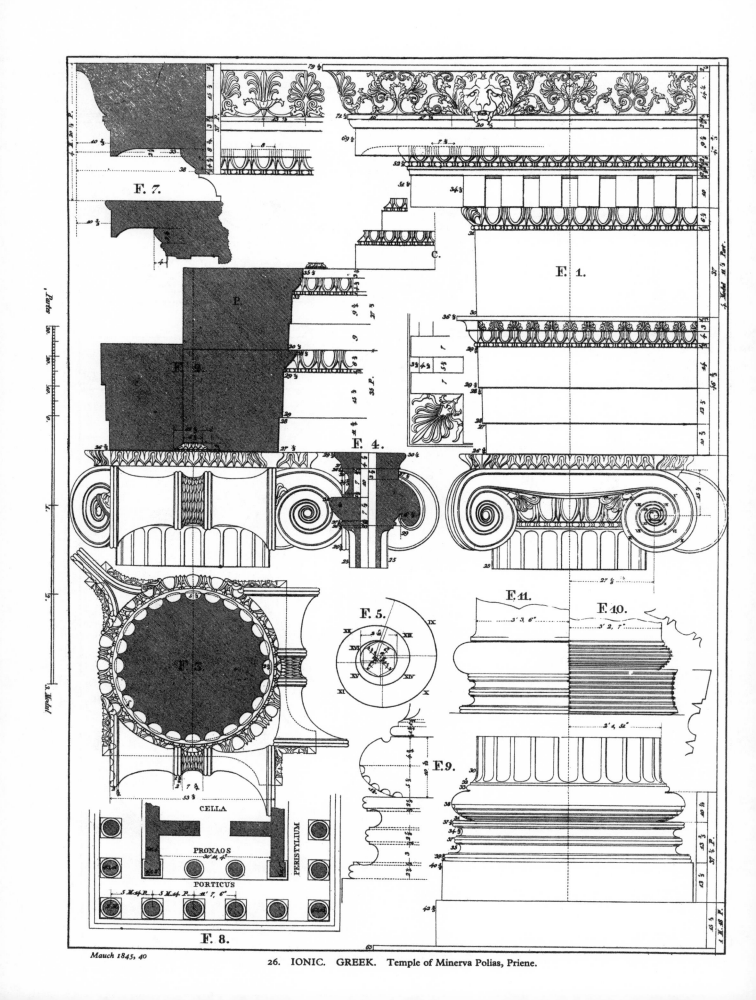

F. 7.

C.

F. 1.

P.

F. 2.

F. 4.

F. 5.

F. 11.

F. 10.

F. 3.

F. 9.

CELLA

PRONAOS

PERISTYLIUM

PORTICUS

F. 8.

Mauch 1845, 40

26. IONIC. GREEK. Temple of Minerva Polias, Priene.

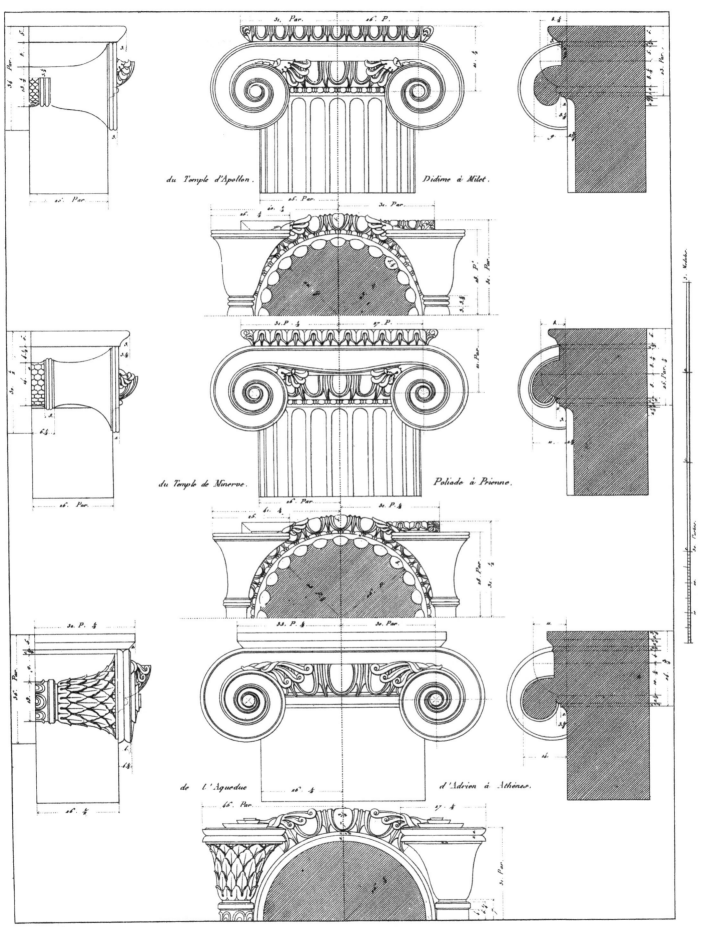

du Temple d'Apollon.

Didime à Milet.

du Temple de Minerve.

Poliade à Prienne.

de l'Aqueduc

d'Adrien à Athènes.

27. IONIC. GREEK. Various capitals. (See Index.)

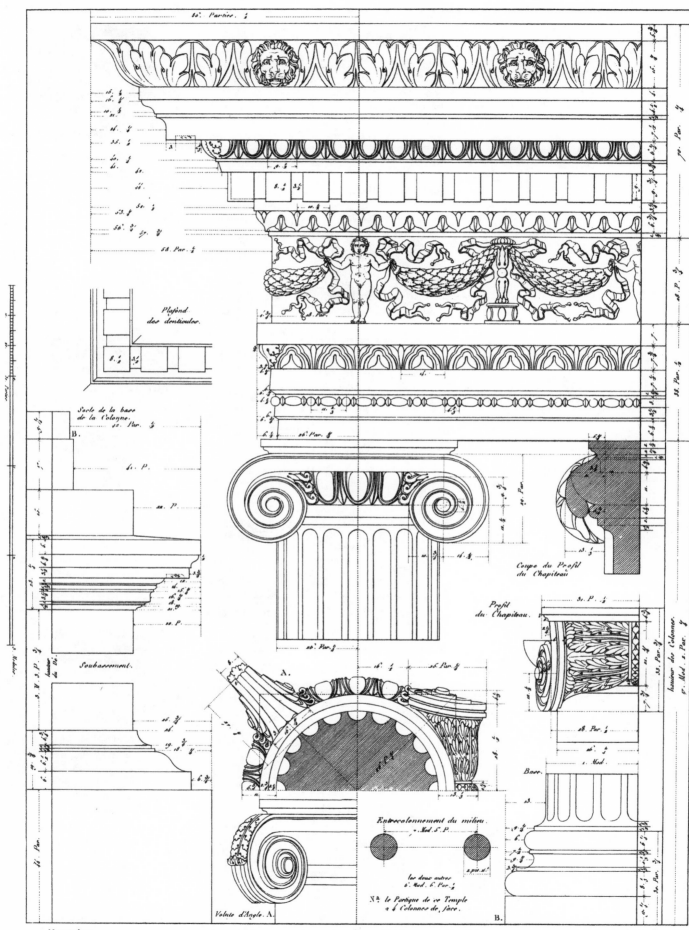

Plafond
des denticules.

Socle de la base
de la Colonne.

Soubassement.

Coupe du Profil
du Chapiteau

Profil
du Chapiteau.

Entrecolonnement du milieu.

les deux autres

N?. le Portique de ce Temple
a 4 Colonnes de face.

Volute d'Angle. A.

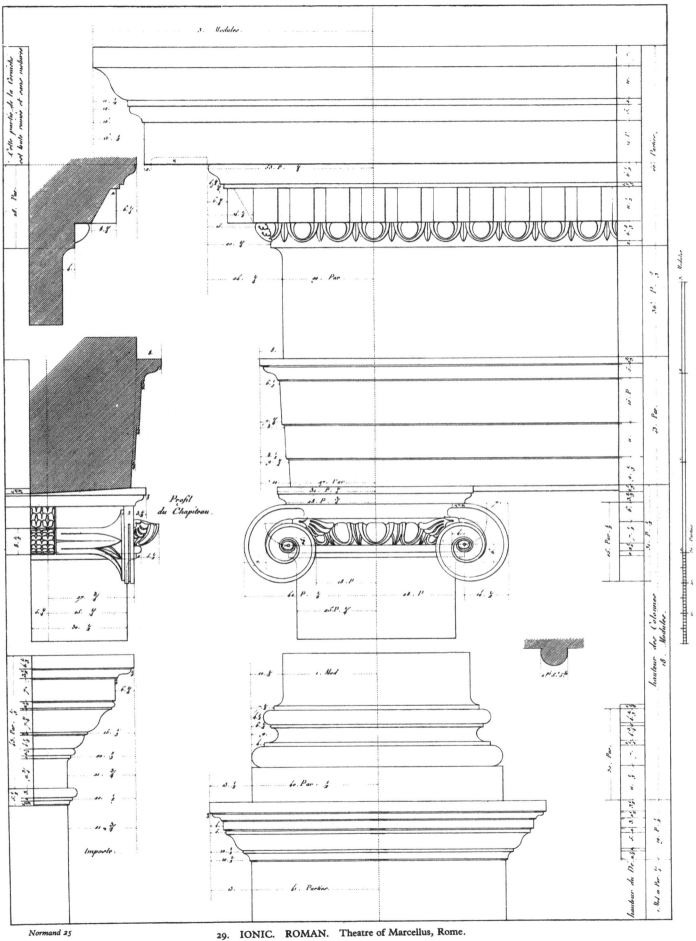

Profil
du Chapiteau.

Imposte.

29. IONIC. ROMAN. Theatre of Marcellus, Rome.

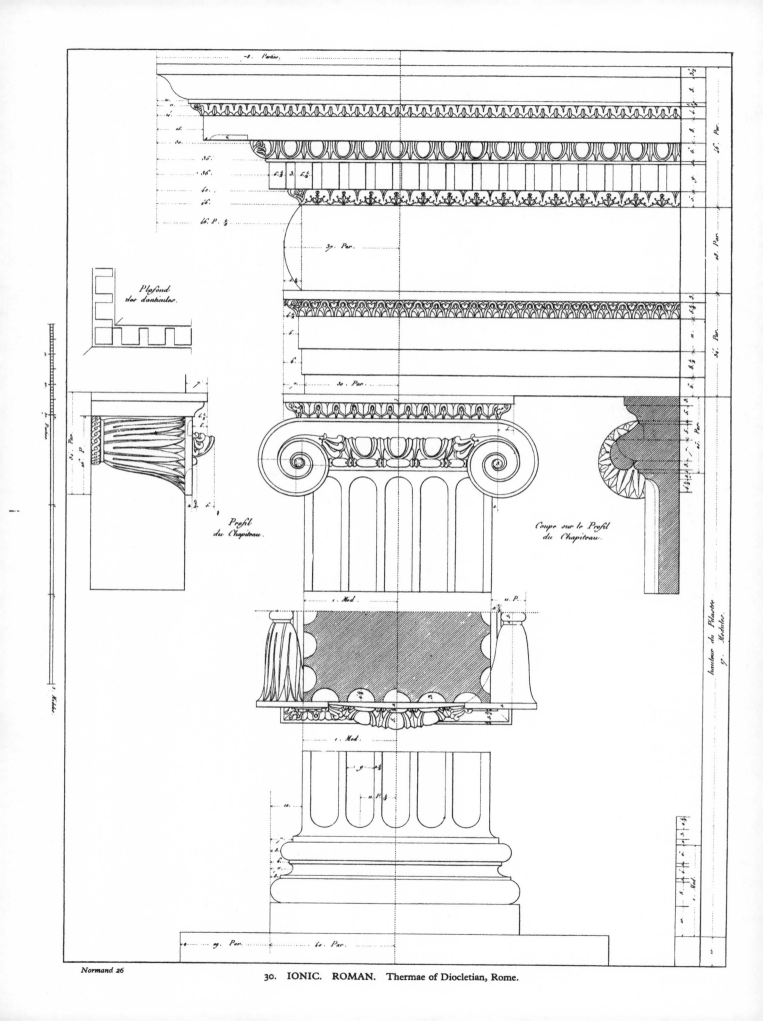

Plafond
des denticules.

Profil
du Chapiteau.

Coupe sur le Profil
du Chapiteau.

30. IONIC. ROMAN. Thermae of Diocletian, Rome.

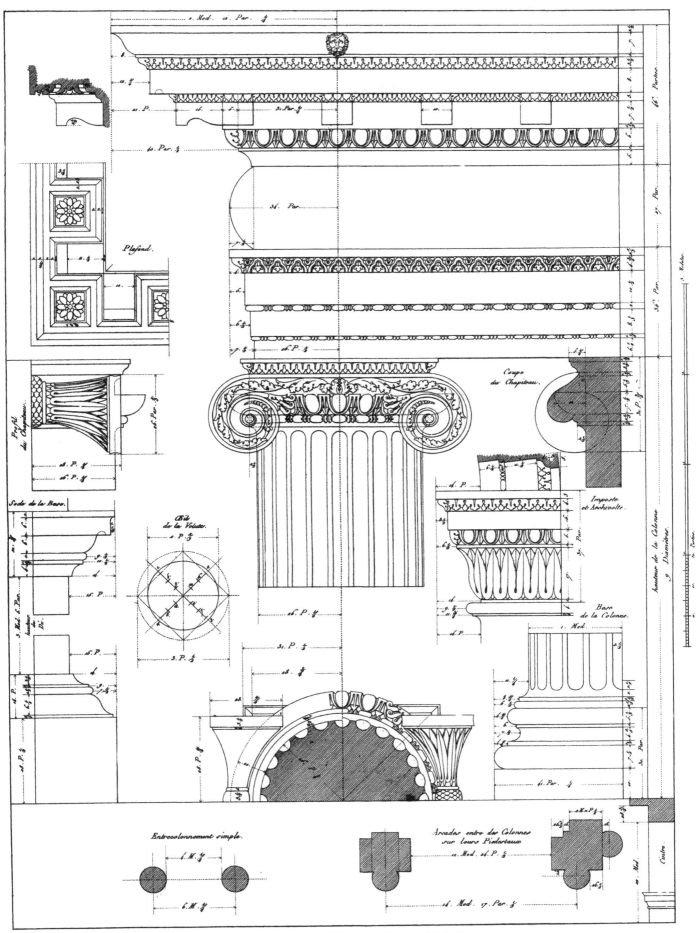

Plafond.

Profil du Chapiteau.

Socle de la Base.

Œil de la Volute.

Coupe du Chapiteau.

Imposte et Archivolte.

Base de la Colonne.

hauteur de la Colonne 9 Diamètres.

Cintre.

Entrecolonnement simple.

Arcades entre des Colonnes sur leurs Piédestaux.

31. IONIC. RENAISSANCE. Version of Palladio.

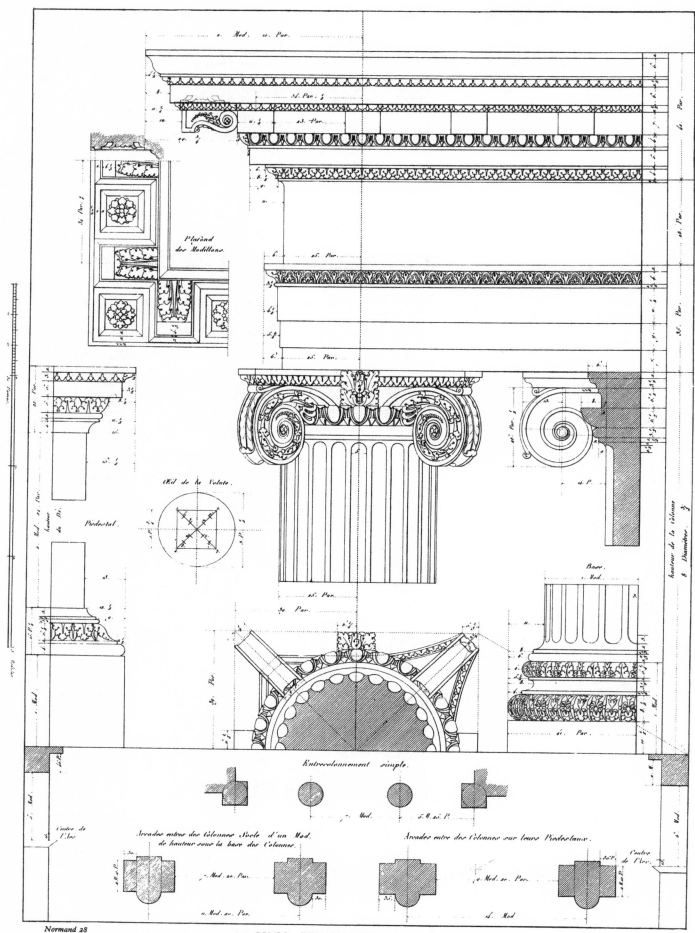

Plafond des Modillons.

Œil de la Volute.

Piédestal.

Base.

Entrecolonnement simple.

Arcades entres des Colonnes Socle d'un Mod. de hauteur sous la base des Colonnes.

Arcades entre des Colonnes sur leurs Piédestaux.

32. IONIC. RENAISSANCE. Version of Scamozzi.

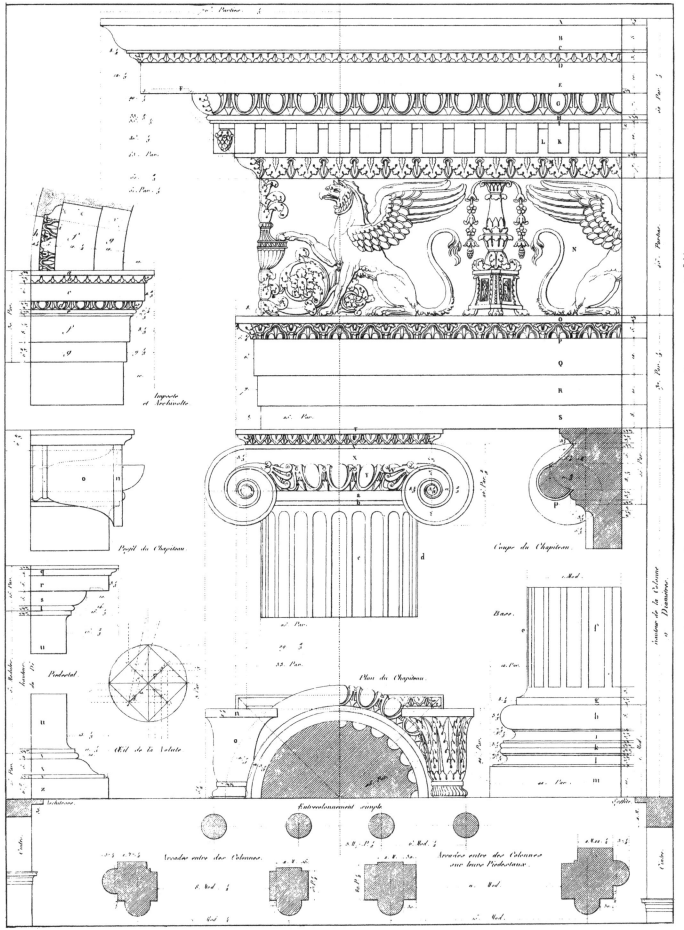

33. IONIC. RENAISSANCE. Version of Vignola.

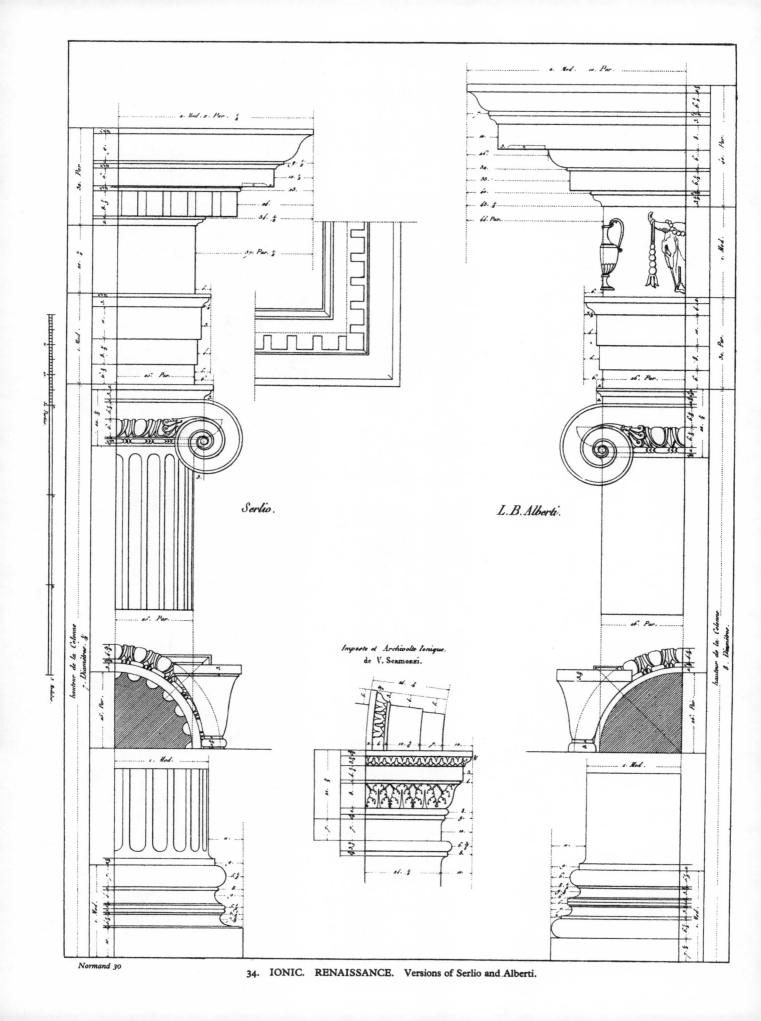

Serlio.

L.B.Alberti.

Imposte et Archivolte Ionique.
de V. Scamozzi.

34. IONIC. RENAISSANCE. Versions of Serlio and Alberti.

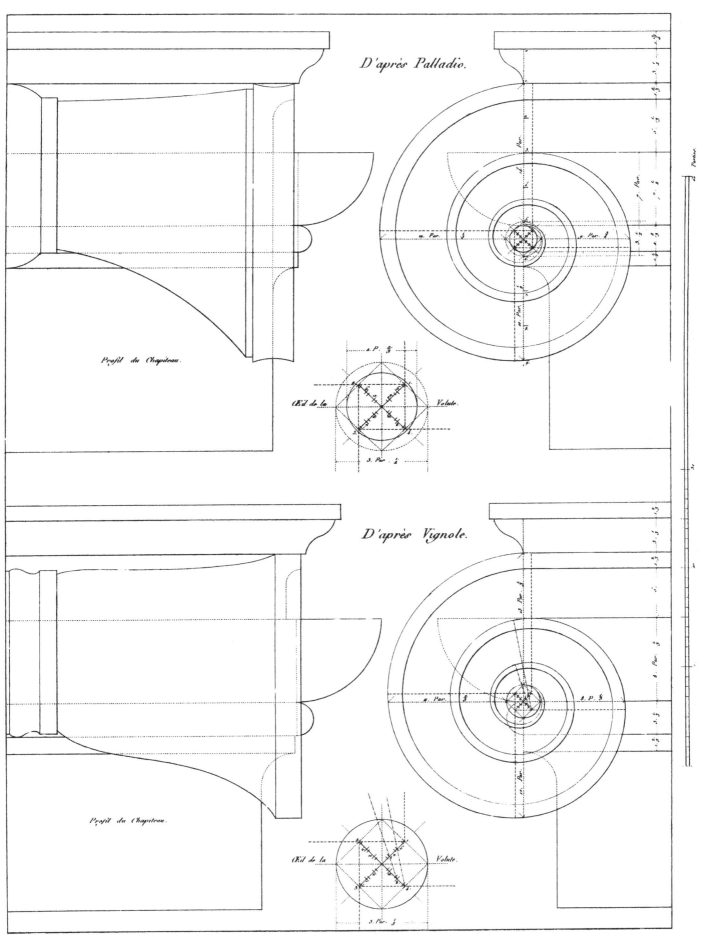

D'après Palladio.

Profil du Chapiteau.

Œil de la   *Volute.*

D'après Vignole.

Profil du Chapiteau.

Œil de la   *Volute.*

35. IONIC. RENAISSANCE. Setting-out of volutes according to Palladio and Vignola.

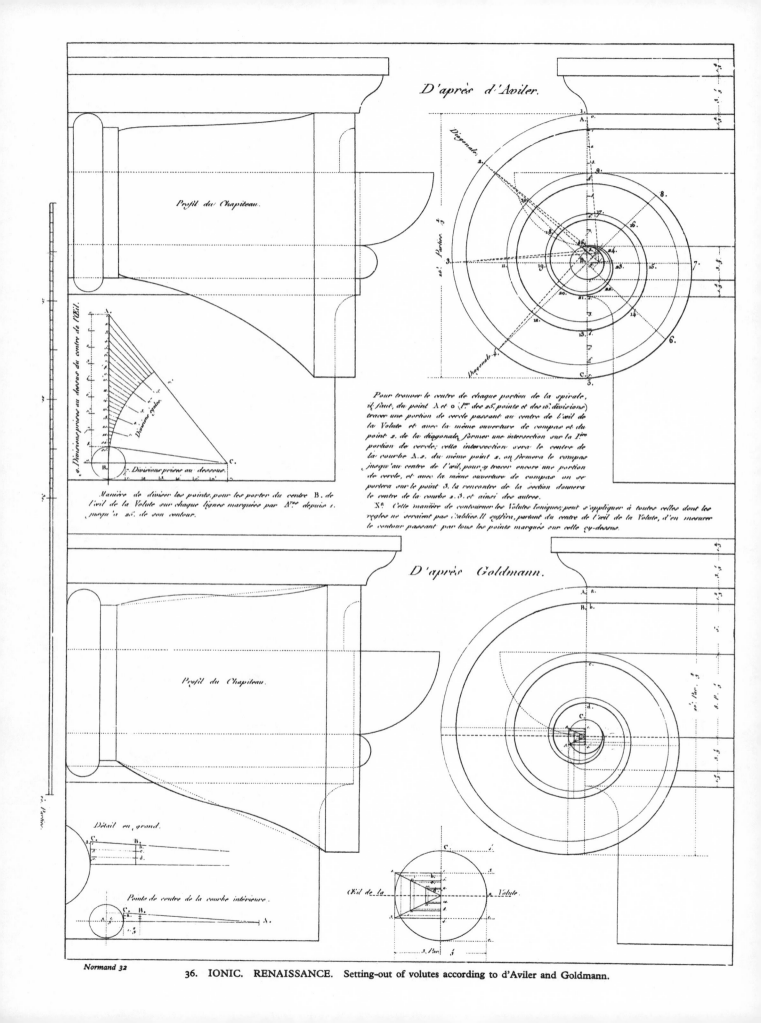

D'après d'Aviler.

Profil du Chapiteau.

Diagonale.

Pour trouver le centre de chaque portion de la spirale, il faut, du point A et o (I.er des 25 points et des 10 divisions) tracer une portion de cercle passant au centre de l'œil de la Volute et avec la même ouverture de compas et du point 2 de la diagonale former une intersection sur la 1.ere portion de cercle; cette intersection sera le centre de la courbe A.2. du même point 2, on formera le compas jusqu'au centre de l'œil, pour y tracer encore une portion de cercle, et avec la même ouverture de compas on se portera sur le point 3. la rencontre de la section donnera le centre de la courbe 2.3. et ainsi des autres.

N.a Cette manière de contourner les Volutes Ioniques; peut s'appliquer à toutes celles dont les regles ne seraient pas établies. Il suffira, partant du centre de l'œil de la Volute, d'en mesurer le contour passant par tous les points marqués sur celle cy-dessus.

Manière de diviser les points, pour les porter du centre B. de l'œil de la Volute sur chaque lignes marquées par N.os depuis 1 jusqu'à 25 de son contour.

D'après Goldmann.

Profil du Chapiteau.

Détail en grand.

Points de centre de la courbe intérieure.

Œil de la Volute.

36. IONIC. RENAISSANCE. Setting-out of volutes according to d'Aviler and Goldmann.

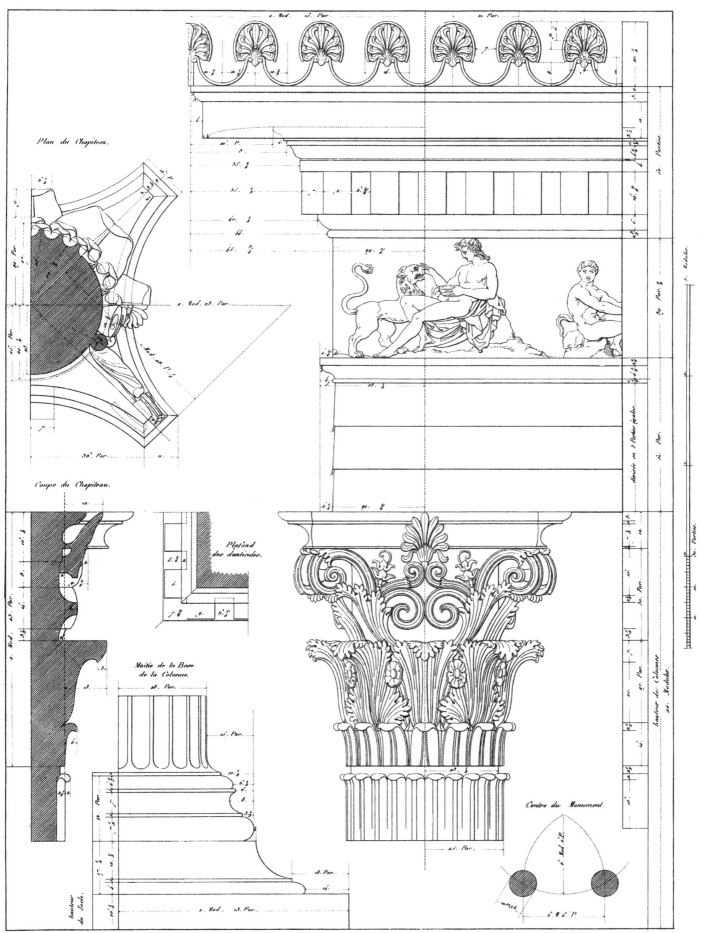

Plan du Chapiteau.

Coupe du Chapiteau.

Plafond
des denticules.

Moitié de la Base
de la Colonne.

Centre du Monument.

37. CORINTHIAN. GREEK. Monument of Lysicrates, Athens.

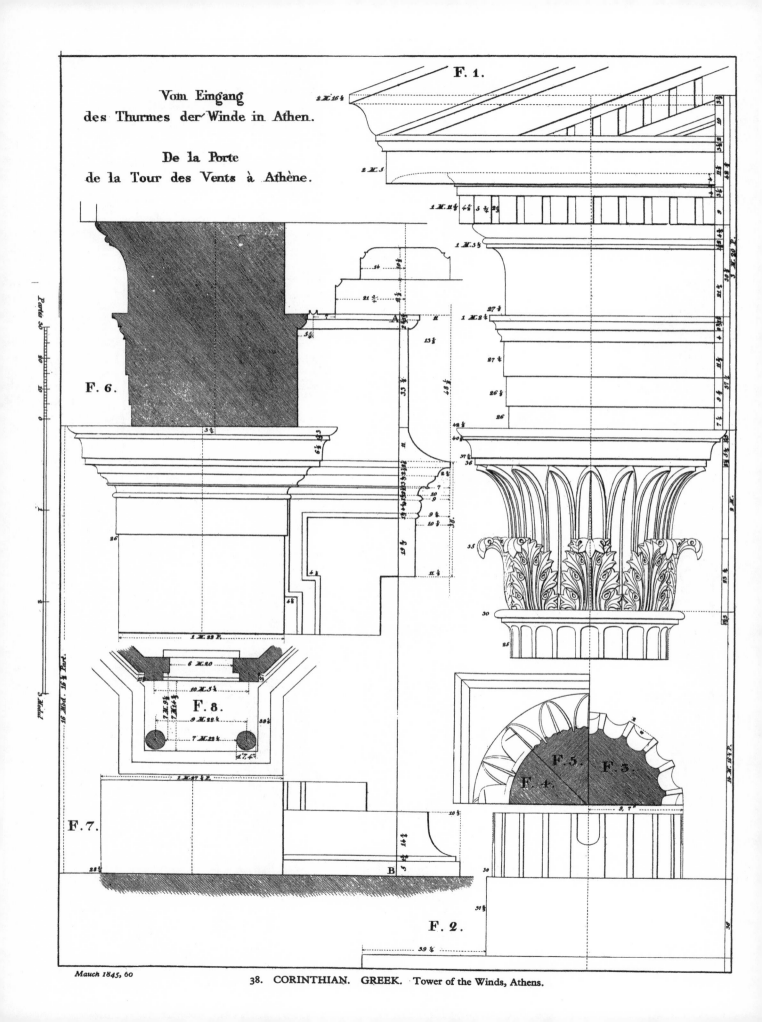

F. 1.

Vom Eingang
des Thurmes der Winde in Athen.

De la Porte
de la Tour des Vents à Athène.

F. 6.

F. 8.

F. 7.

F. 5.

F. 4.

F. 3.

F. 2.

Parts 30

Mauch 1845, 60

38. CORINTHIAN. GREEK. Tower of the Winds, Athens.

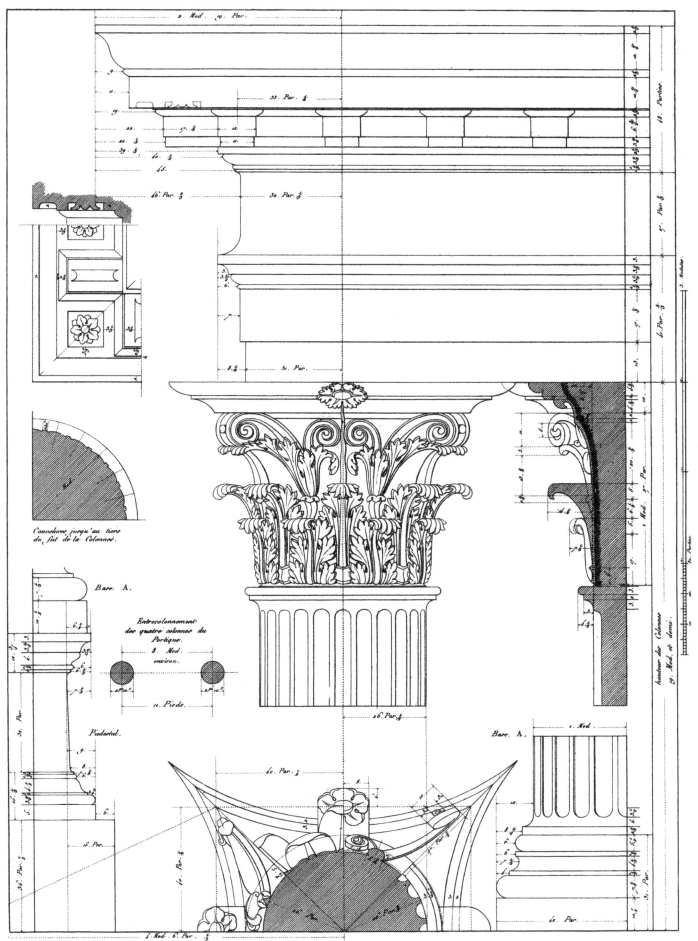

Cannelures jusqu'au tiers
du fut de la Colonne.

Base. A.

Entrecolonnement
des quatre colonnes du
Portique.
8. Mod.
environ.

11. Pieds.

Piedestal.

Base. A.

hauteur des Colonnes
19. Mod. et demi.

39. CORINTHIAN. GRAECO-ROMAN. Temple of Jupiter Olympius, Athens.

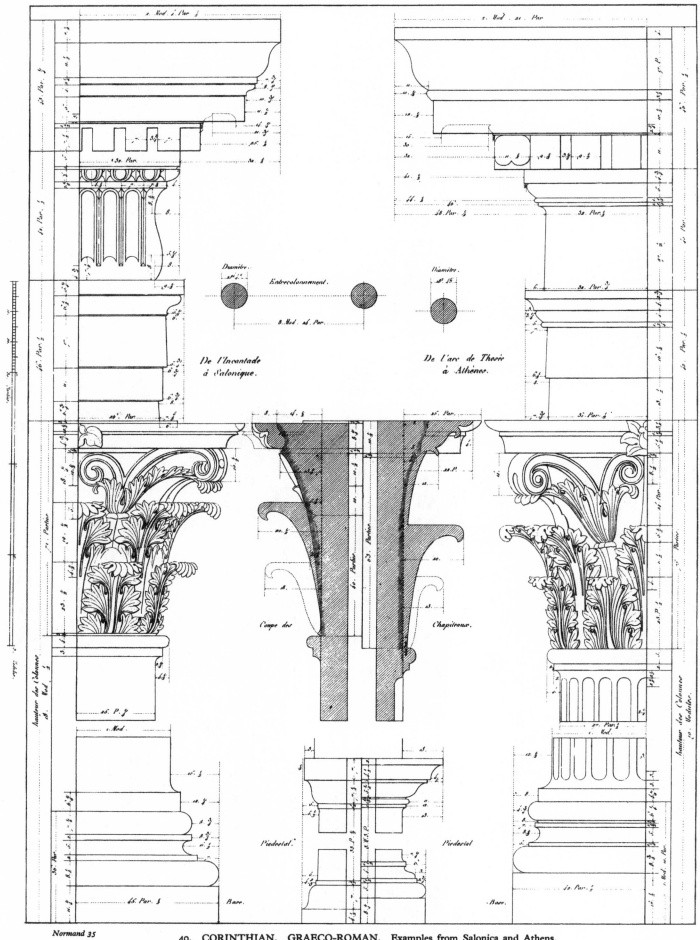

De l'Incantade
à Salonique.

De l'arc de Thesée
à Athènes.

Entrecolonnement.

Coupe des

Chapiteaux.

Piedestal.

Piedestal.

Base.

Base.

40. CORINTHIAN. GRAECO-ROMAN. Examples from Salonica and Athens.

Section from A to A

Side Elevation
of the Volute

Lower Diam.
Upper Diam.
Height of the Col.

Plan at b

Base

Stylobate

Radius 21 F.

Plan at B   Plan at C

Plan at A   Plan at D

30 Min   2   3   Modules

12 In   2   3   English F.

41. CORINTHIAN. ROMAN. Temple of Vesta, Tivoli.

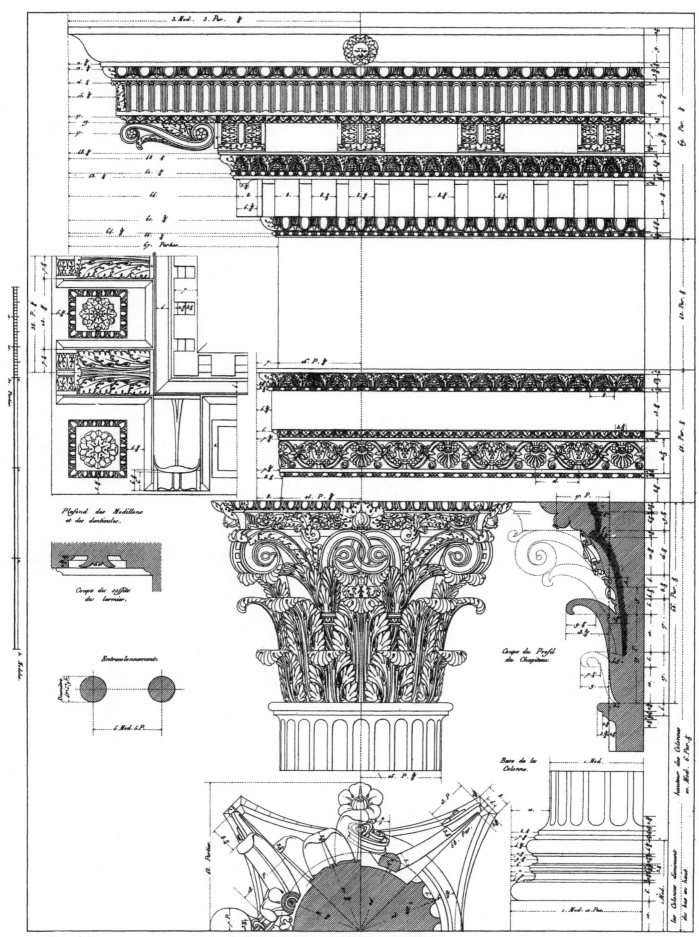

Plafond des Modillons
et des denticules.

Coupe du soffite
du larmier.

Entrecolonnement.

Coupe du Profil
du Chapiteau.

Base de la
Colonne.

42. CORINTHIAN. ROMAN. Temple of Castor and Pollux, Rome.

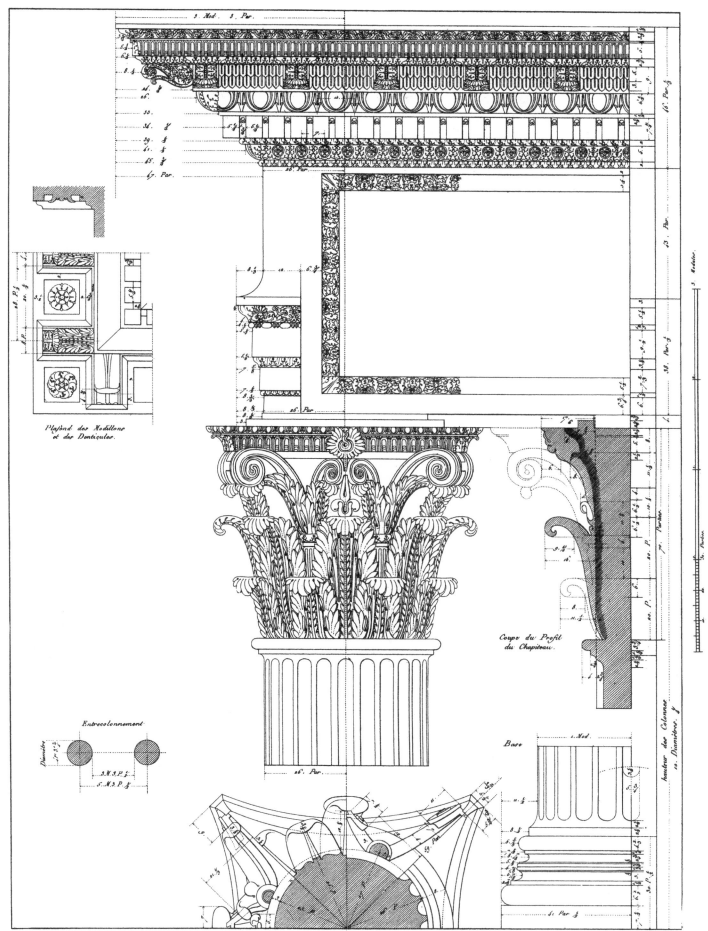

Plafond des Modillons
et des Denticules.

Coupe du Profil
du Chapiteau.

Base

Entrecolonnement

Normand 37

43. CORINTHIAN. ROMAN. Temple of Vespasian, Rome.

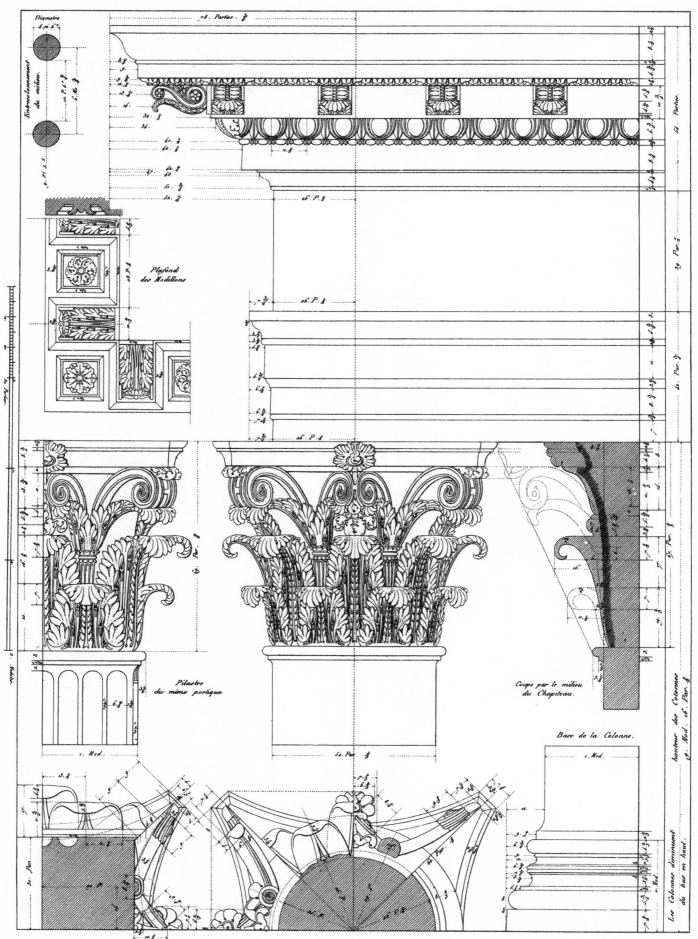

Diametre

Entrevlement du milieu

Plafond des Modillons

Pilastre du même portique.

Coupe par le milieu du Chapiteau.

Base de la Colonne.

44.   CORINTHIAN. ROMAN. Portico of the Pantheon, Rome.

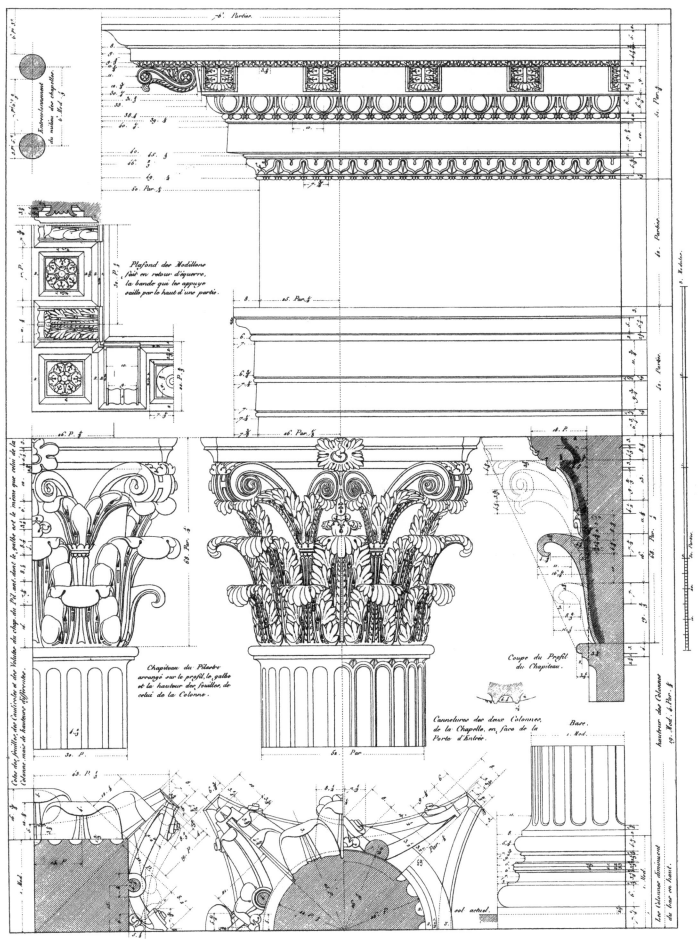

45. CORINTHIAN. ROMAN. Interior order of the Pantheon, Rome.

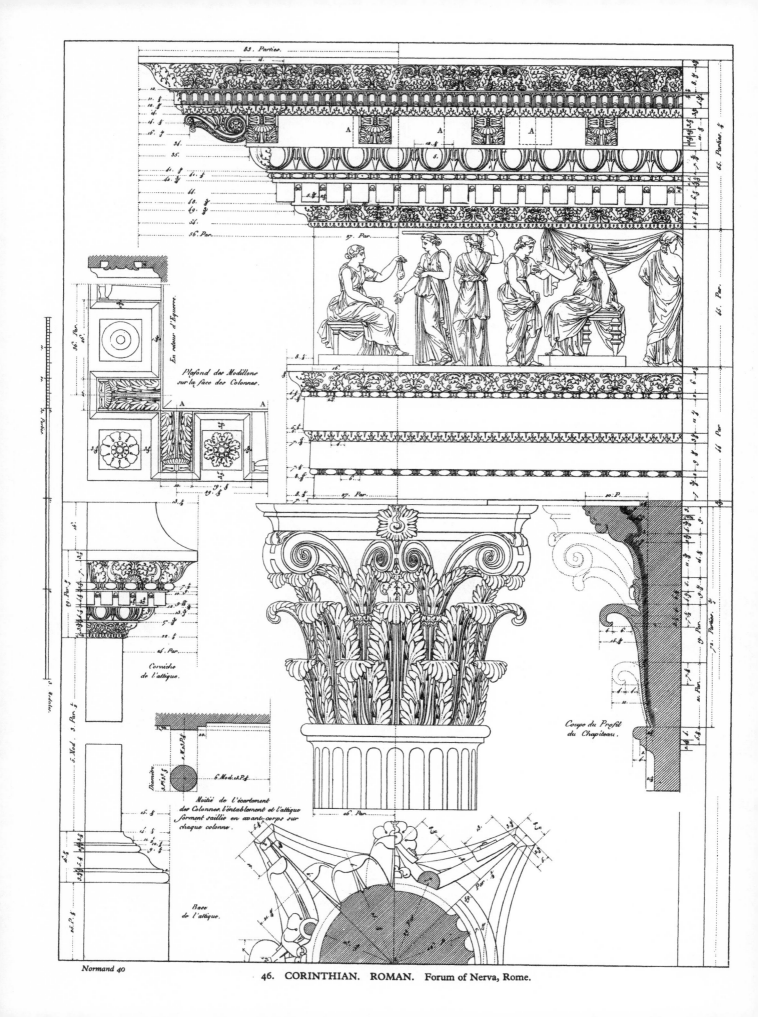

Plafond des Modillons
sur la face des Colonnes.

En retour d'Equerre.

Corniche
de l'attique.

Moitié de l'écartement
des Colonnes. l'entablement et l'attique
forment saillie en avant-corps sur
chaque colonne.

Coupe du Profil
du Chapiteau.

Base
de l'attique.

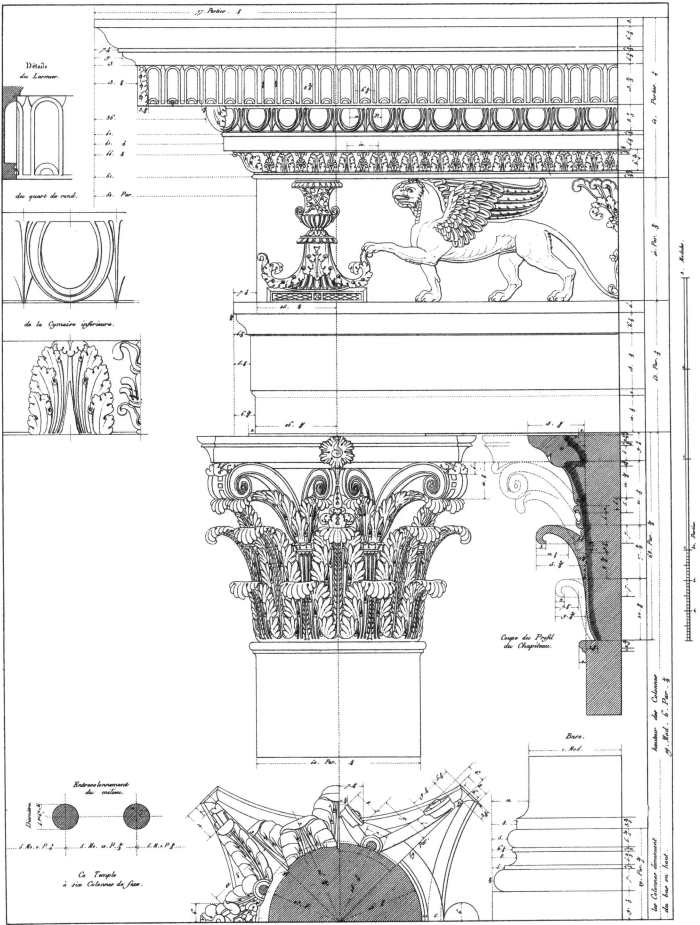

47. CORINTHIAN. ROMAN. Temple of Antoninus and Faustina, Rome.

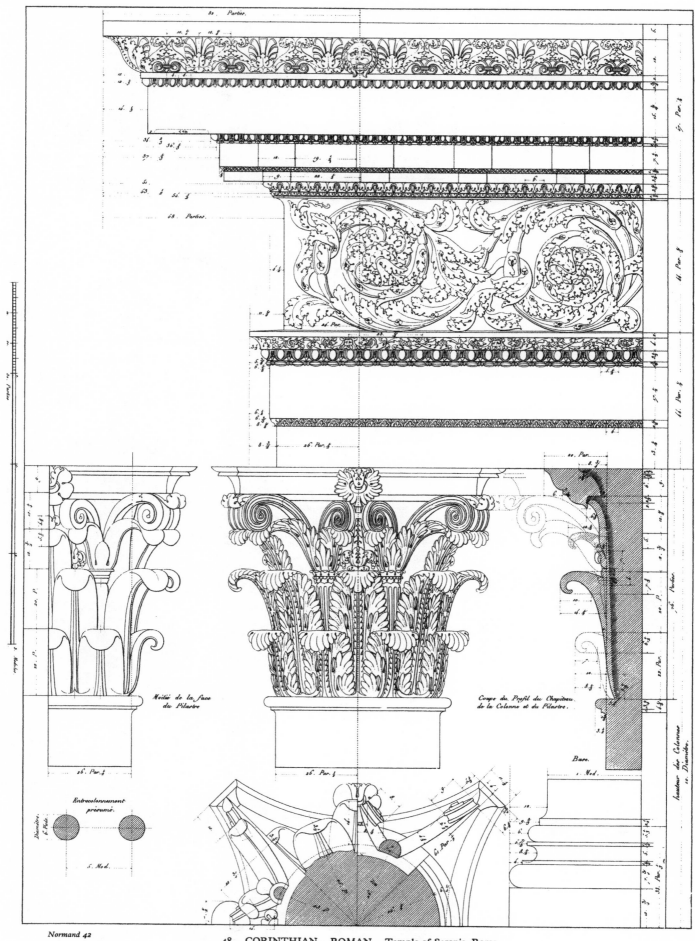

Moitié de la face
du Pilastre

Coupe du Profil du Chapiteau
de la Colonne et du Pilastre.

Base.

Entrecolonnement
présumé.

48. CORINTHIAN. ROMAN. Temple of Serapis, Rome.

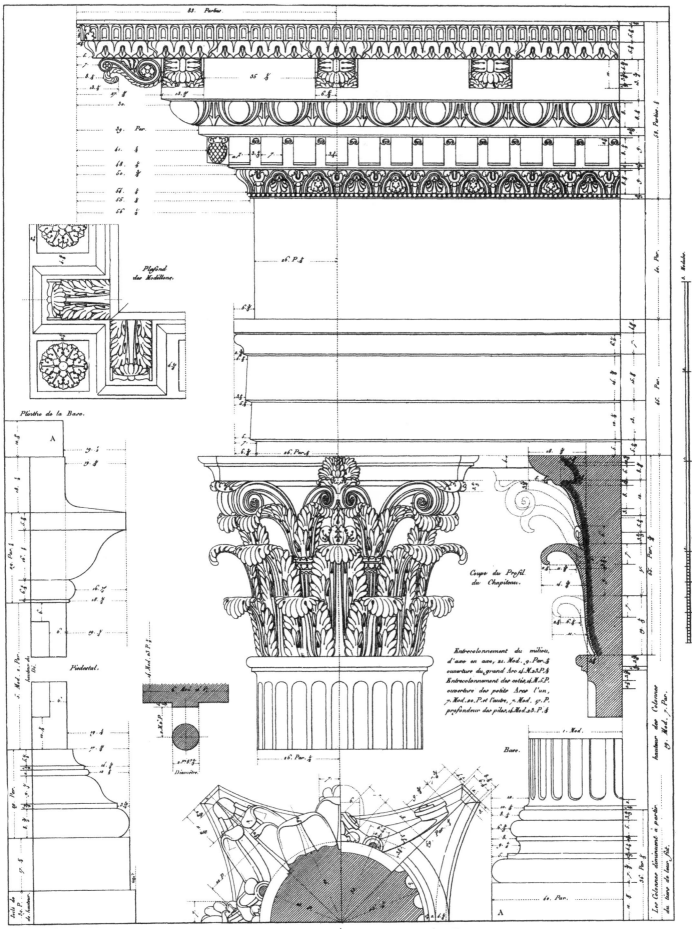

Plafond
des Modillons.

Plinthe de la Base.

A

Piédestal.

Coupe du Profil
du Chapiteau.

Entrecolonnement du milieu,
d'axe en axe, 21. Mod. 9. Par. ½
ouverture du grand Arc 14. M. 3. P. ½
Entrecolonnement des cotés, 14. M. 5. P.
ouverture des petits Arcs l'un,
7. Mod. 20. P. et l'autre, 7. Mod. 17. P.
profondeur des piles, 14. Mod. 23. P. ½

Diamètre.

Base.

A

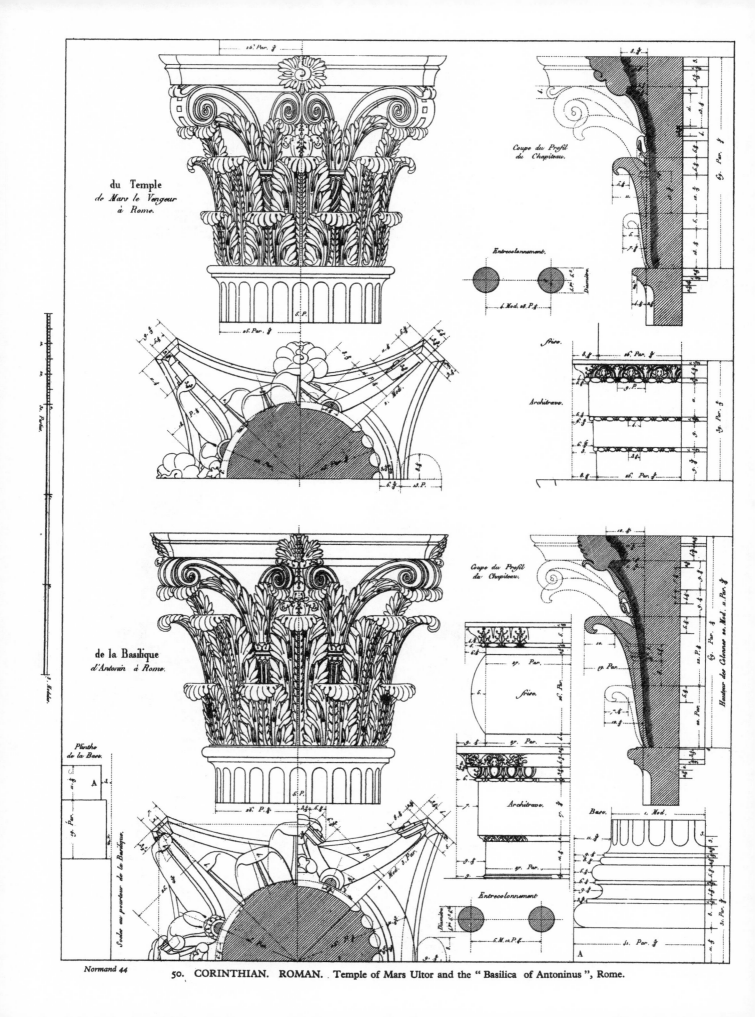

du Temple
*de Mars le Vengeur
à Rome.*

Coupe du Profil
du Chapiteau.

Entrecolonnement.

Frise.

Architrave.

de la Basilique
d'Antonin à Rome.

Coupe du Profil
du Chapiteau.

frise.

Architrave.

Base.

Plinthe
de la Base.

Entrecolonnement

50. CORINTHIAN. ROMAN. Temple of Mars Ultor and the " Basilica of Antoninus ", Rome.

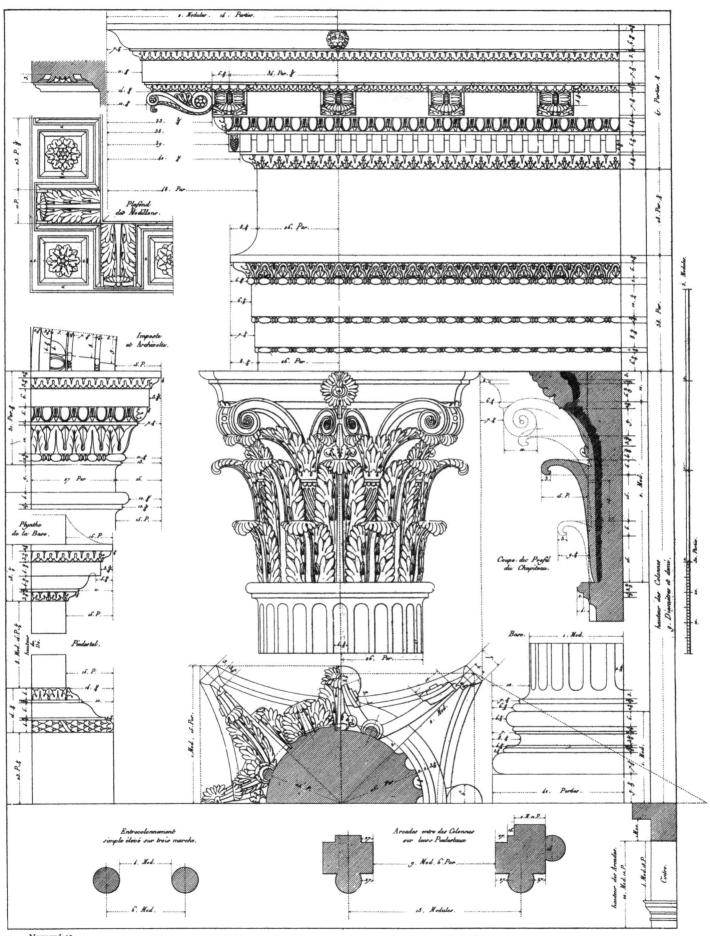

Plafond
des Modillons.

Imposte
et Archivolte.

Plynthe
de la Base.

Piédestal.

Coupe du Profil
du Chapiteau.

Base.

Entrecolonnement
simple élevé sur trois marche.

1. Mod.

6. Mod.

Arcades entre des Colonnes
sur leurs Piédestaux

9. Mod. 6. Par.

13. Modules.

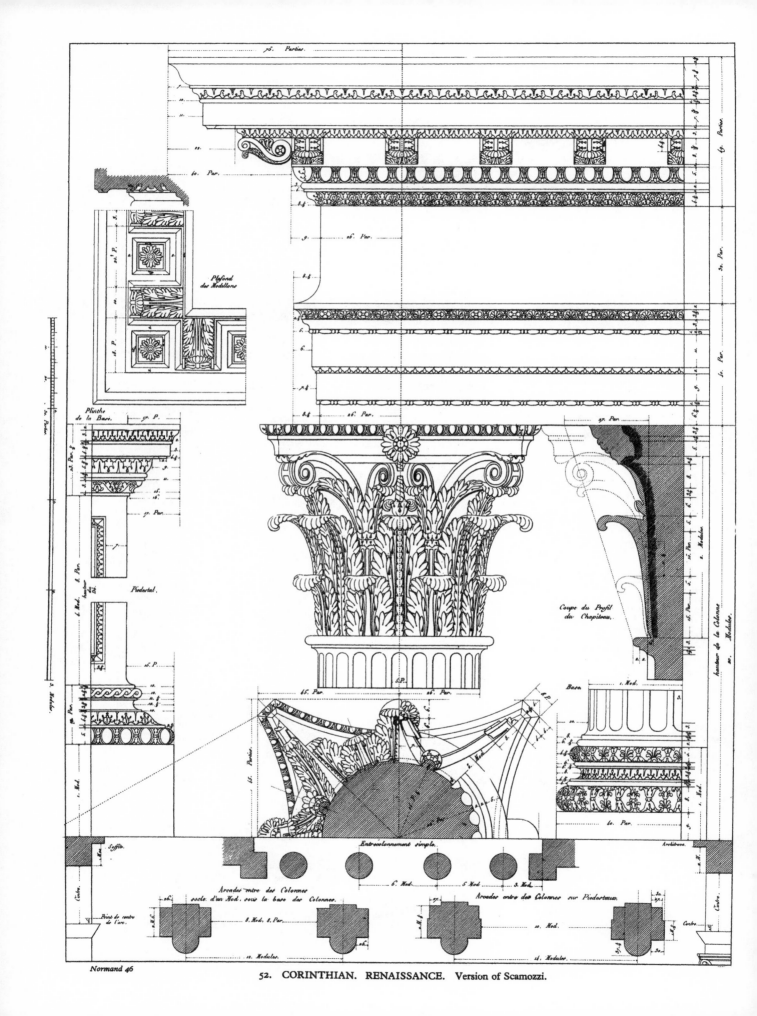

52. CORINTHIAN. RENAISSANCE. Version of Scamozzi.

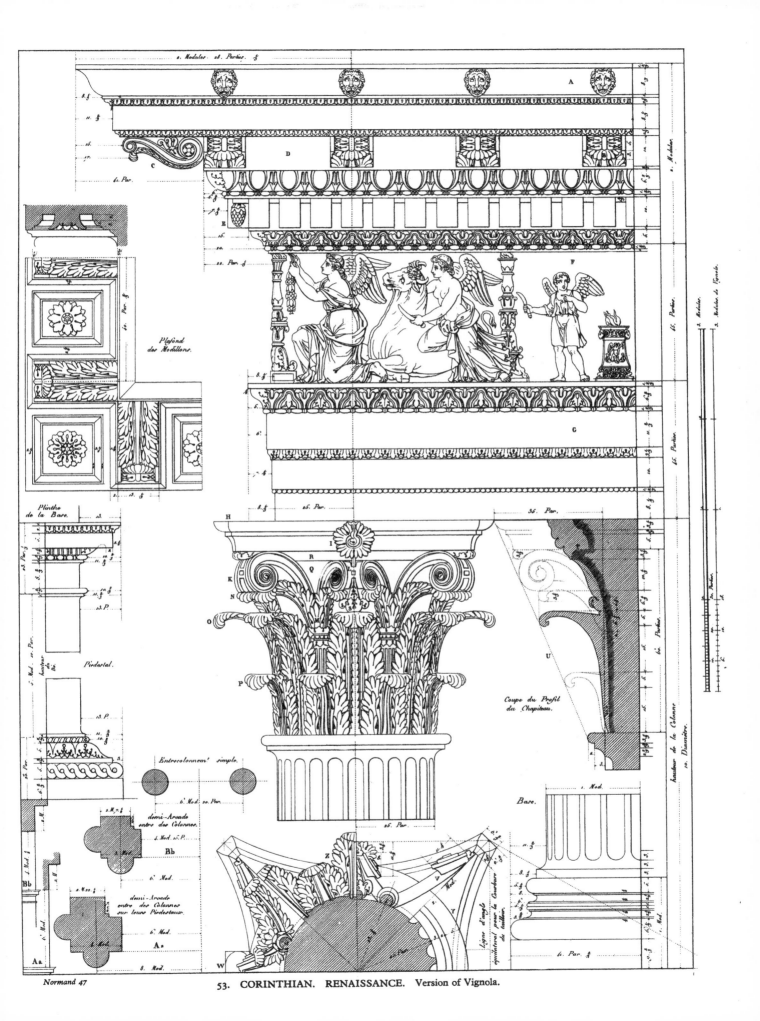

Plafond
des Modillons.

Plinthe
de la Base.

Piedestal.

Entrecolonnem.ᵗ simple.

demi-Arcade
entre des Colonnes.

Bb

demi-Arcade
entre des Colonnes
sur leurs Piédestaux.

Aa

Coupe du Profil
du Chapiteau.

Base.

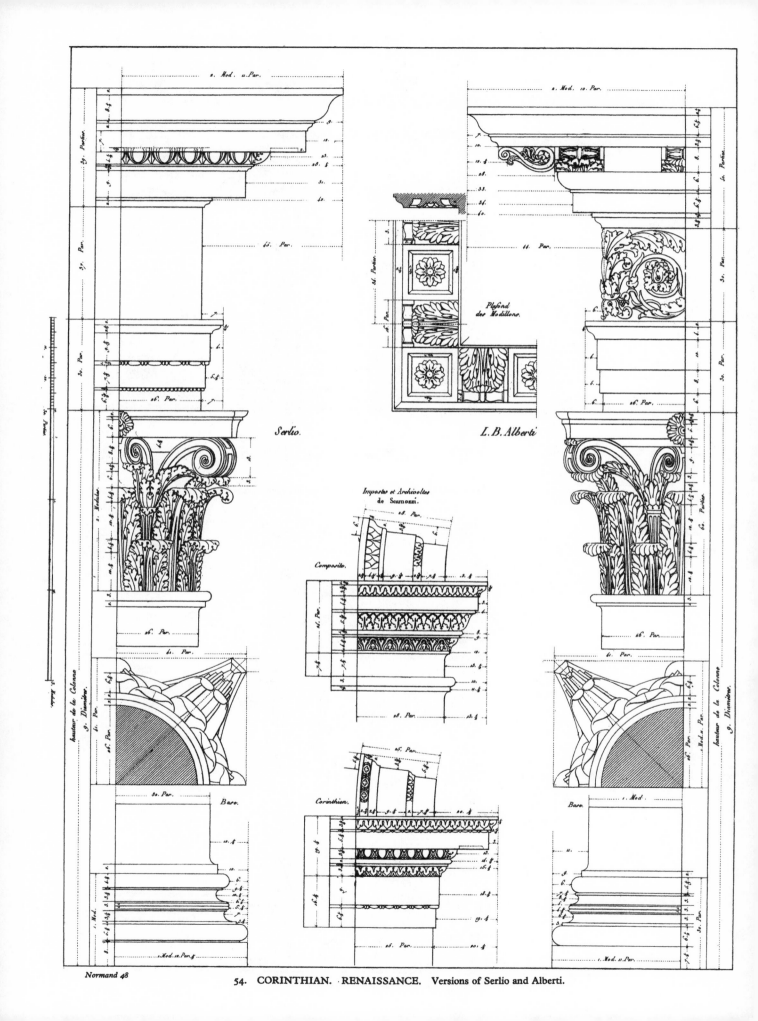

Serlio.

L.B. Alberti

Plafond des Modillons.

Impostes et Archivoltes de Scamozzi.

Composite.

Corinthien.

Base.

Base.

54. CORINTHIAN. RENAISSANCE. Versions of Serlio and Alberti.

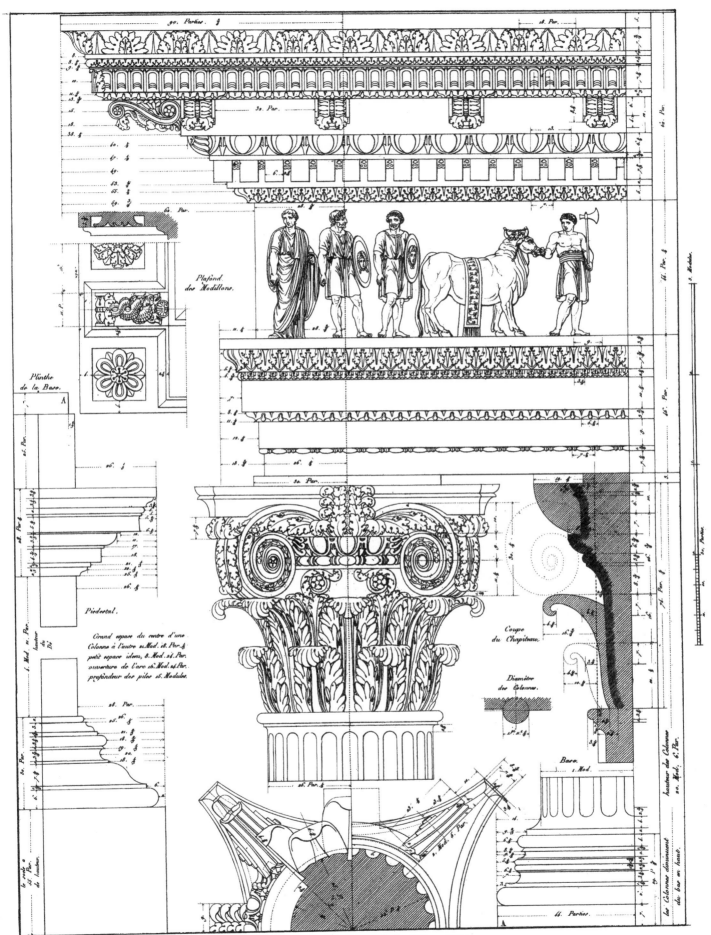

Plafond
des Modillons.

Plinthe
de la Base.

Piédestal.

Grand espace du centre d'une
Colonne à l'autre 21.Mod. 18.Par.¾
petit espace idem. 8.Mod. 24.Par.
ouverture de l'arc 16.Mod. 24.Par.
profondeur des piles 15.Modules.

Coupe
du Chapiteau.

Diamètre
des Colonnes.

Base.
1.Mod.

55. COMPOSITE. ROMAN. Arch of Titus, Rome.

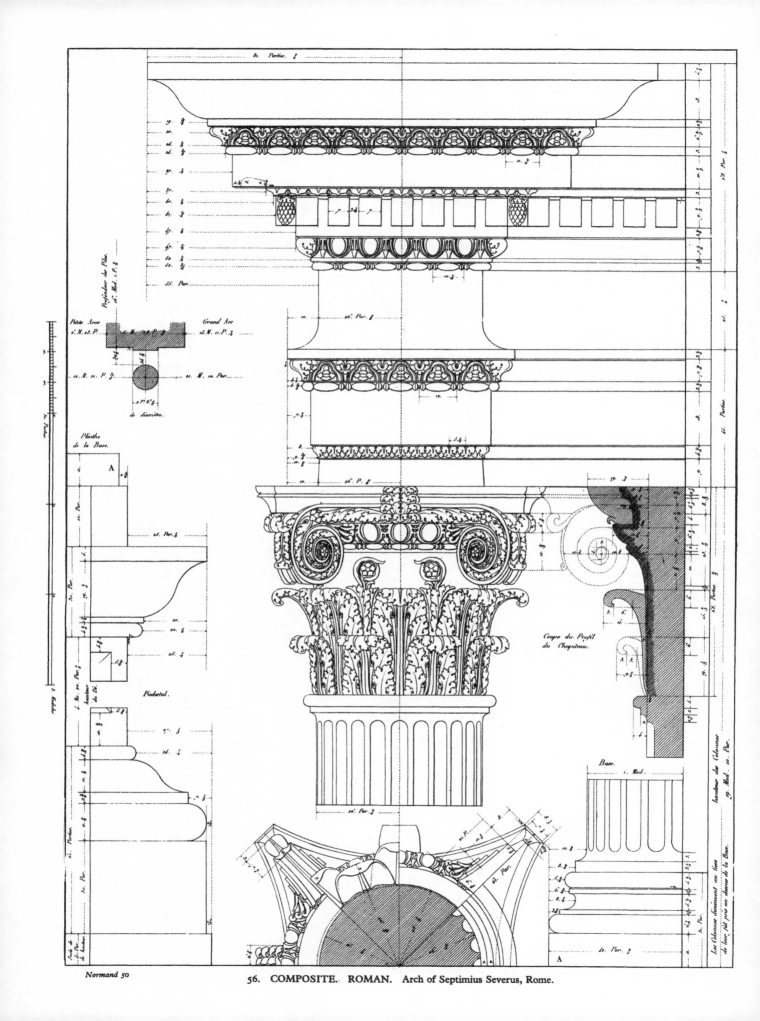

Normand 50

56. COMPOSITE. ROMAN. Arch of Septimius Severus, Rome.

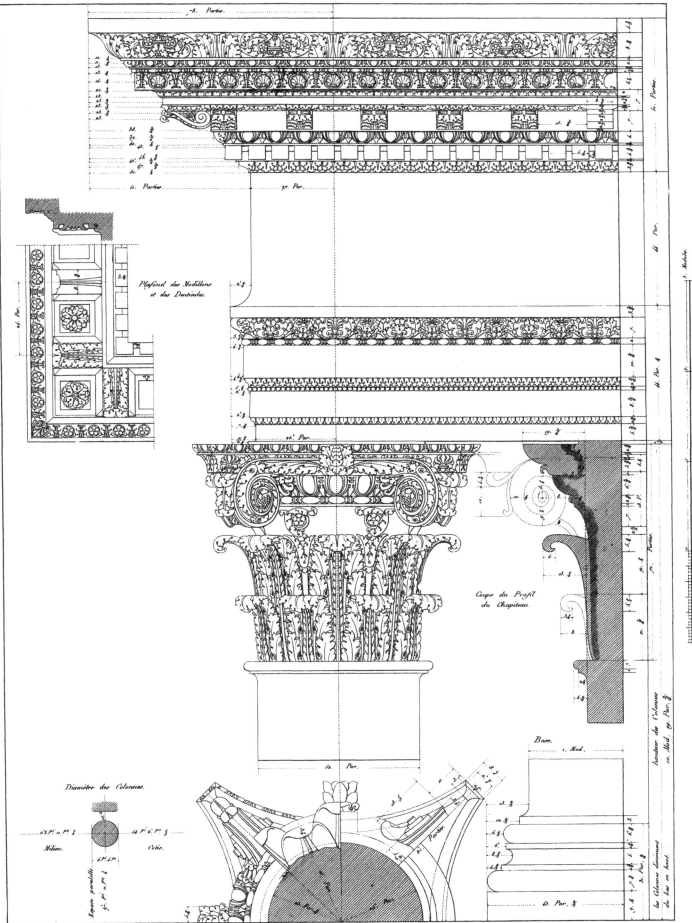

Plafond des Modillons
et des Denticules.

Coupe du Profil
du Chapiteau.

Base.

Diamètre des Colonnes.

57. COMPOSITE. ROMAN. Great Hall of the Thermae of Diocletian, Rome.

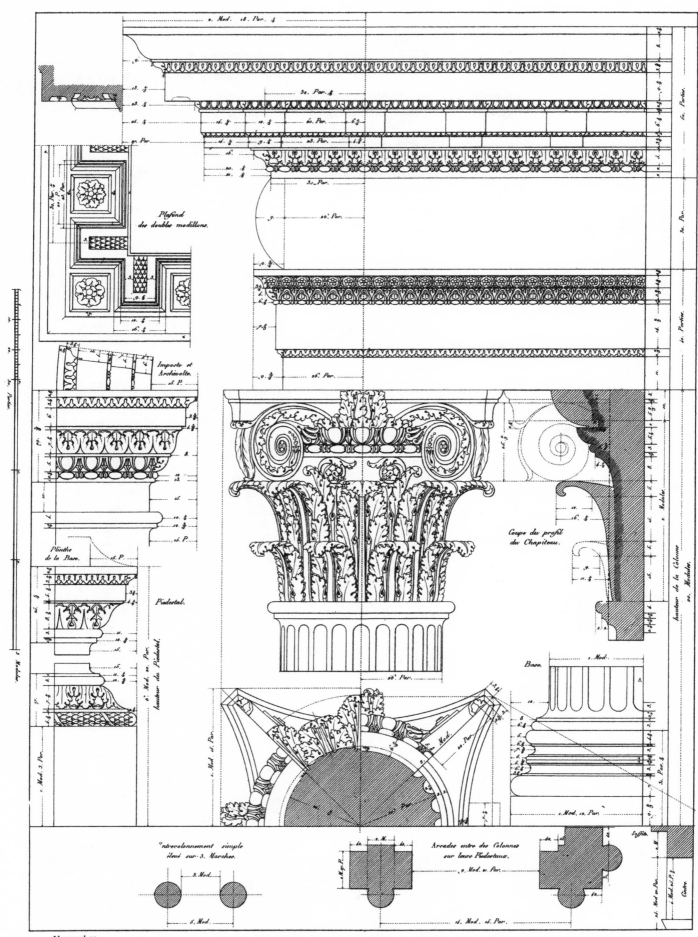

Plafond
des doubles modillons.

Imposte et
Archivolte.
15. P.

Plinthe
de la Base.

Piedestal.

Coupe du profil
du Chapiteau.

Base.

hauteur de la Colonne
20. Modules.

Entrecolonnement simple
élevé sur 3. Marches.

Arcades entre des Colonnes
sur leurs Piedestaux.

Soffite.

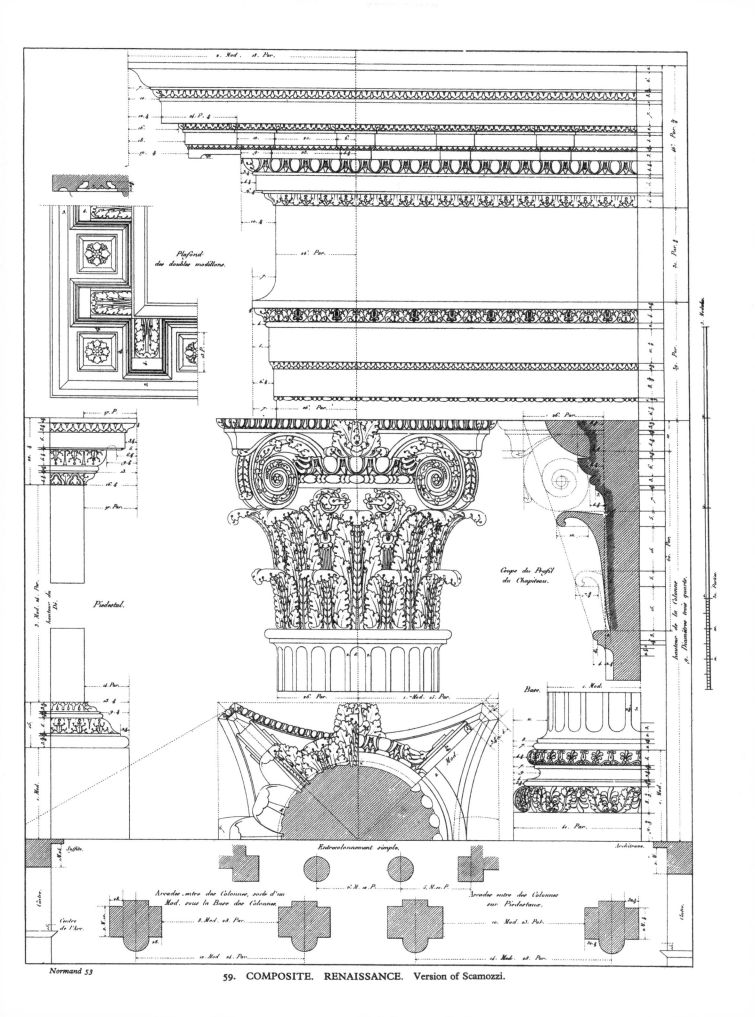

Plafond
des doubles modillons.

Piédestal.

Coupe du Profil
du Chapiteau.

Base.

Entrecolonnement simple.

Arcades entre des Colonnes, socle d'un
Mod. sous la Base des Colonnes.

Arcades entre des Colonnes
sur Piédestaux.

59. COMPOSITE. RENAISSANCE. Version of Scamozzi.

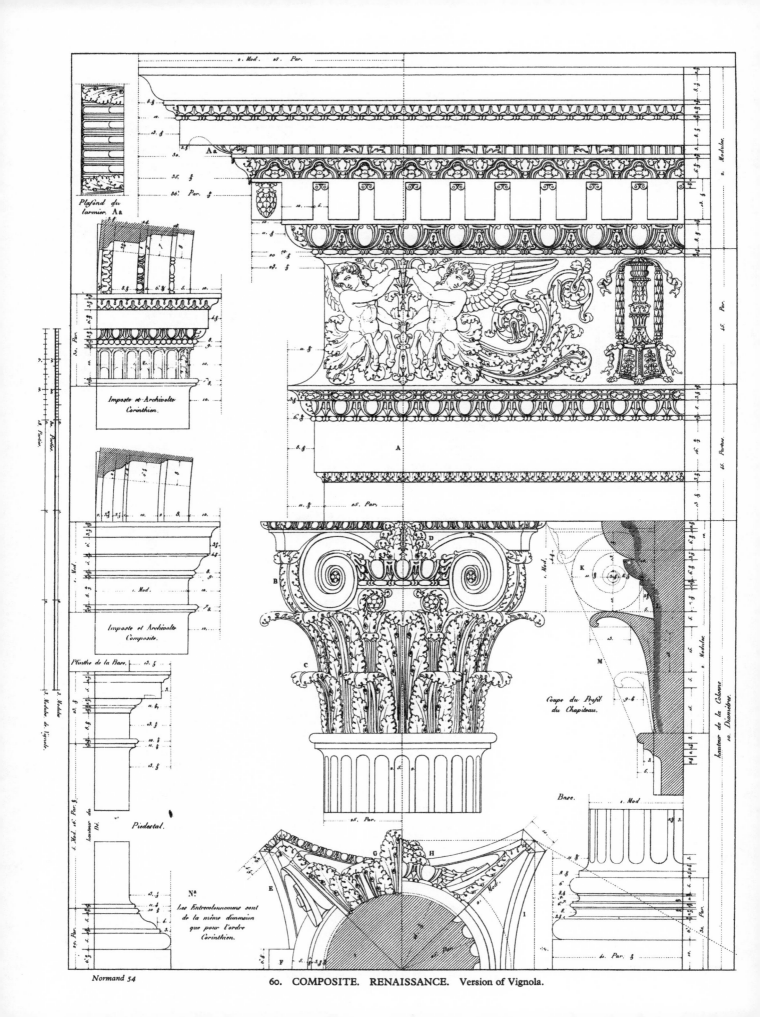

Plafond du
Larmier. Aa

Imposte et Archivolte
Corinthien.

Imposte et Archivolte
Composite.

Plinthe de la Base.

Piedestal.

Coupe du Profil
du Chapiteau.

Base.

Nᵃ
Les Entrecolonnemens sont
de la même dimension
que pour l'ordre
Corinthien.

60. COMPOSITE. RENAISSANCE. Version of Vignola.

Plafond
des Denticules.

Distance d'une
Caryatide à l'autre.

Plinthe de la Caryatide.

Soubassement

Ante.

N⁰. Pour la forme d'une des
Caryatides voyez le frontispice.

N⁰. Il y a au dessous de ce socle deux marches de 30.Par.½
de hauteur, et dont la saillie est de 43. à 45. Parties.

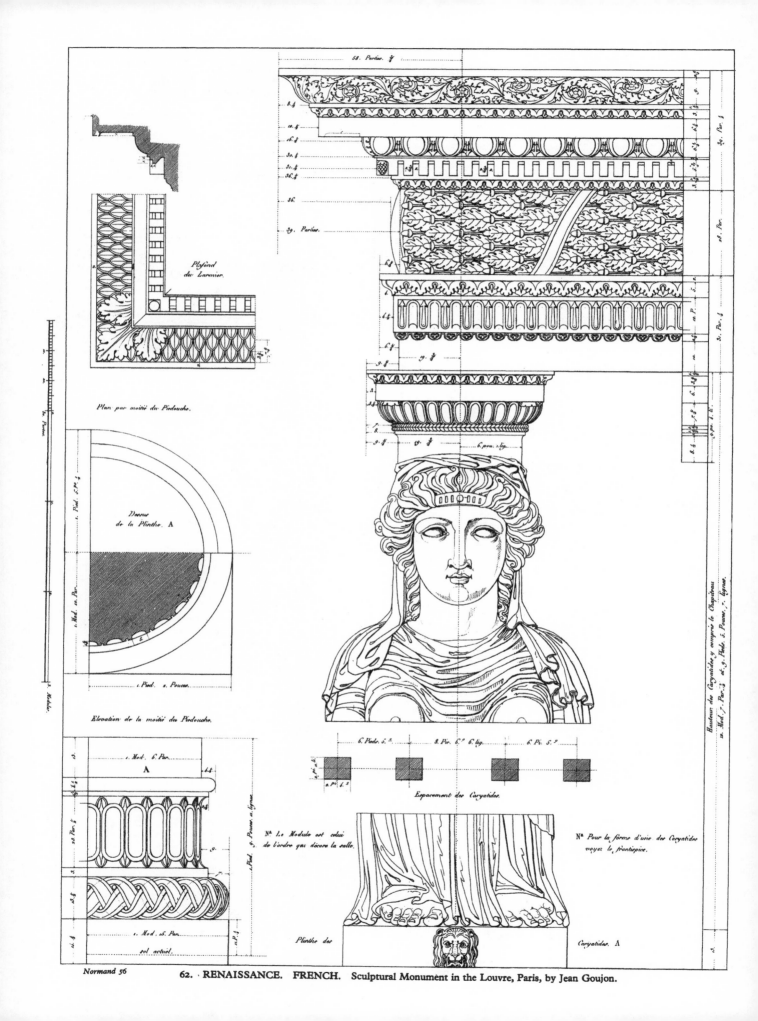

Plafond
du Larmier.

Plan par moitié du Piedouche.

Dessus
de la Plinthe. A

Elevation de la moitié du Piedouche.

A

Espacement des Caryatides.

N.ᵃ Le Module est celui
de l'ordre qui décore la salle.

N.ᵃ Pour la forme d'une des Caryatides
voyez le frontispice.

Plinthe des   Caryatides. A

Normand 56   **62 · RENAISSANCE. FRENCH.** Sculptural Monument in the Louvre, Paris, by Jean Goujon.

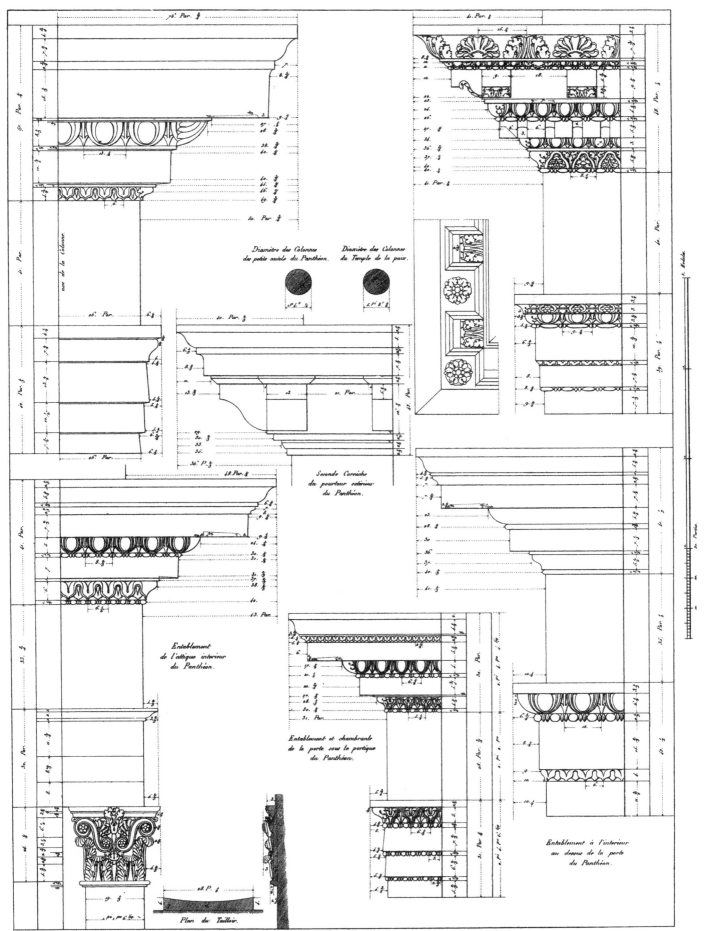

Diamètre des Colonnes
des petits auteb du Panthéon.

Diamètre des Colonnes
du Temple de la paix.

Seconde Corniche
du pourtour extérieur
du Panthéon.

Entablement
de l'attique intérieur
du Panthéon.

Entablement et chambranle
de la porte sous le portique
du Panthéon.

Entablement à l'intérieur
au dessus de la porte
du Panthéon.

Plan du Tailloir.

63. ROMAN ENTABLATURES. Various, mainly from the Pantheon, Rome.

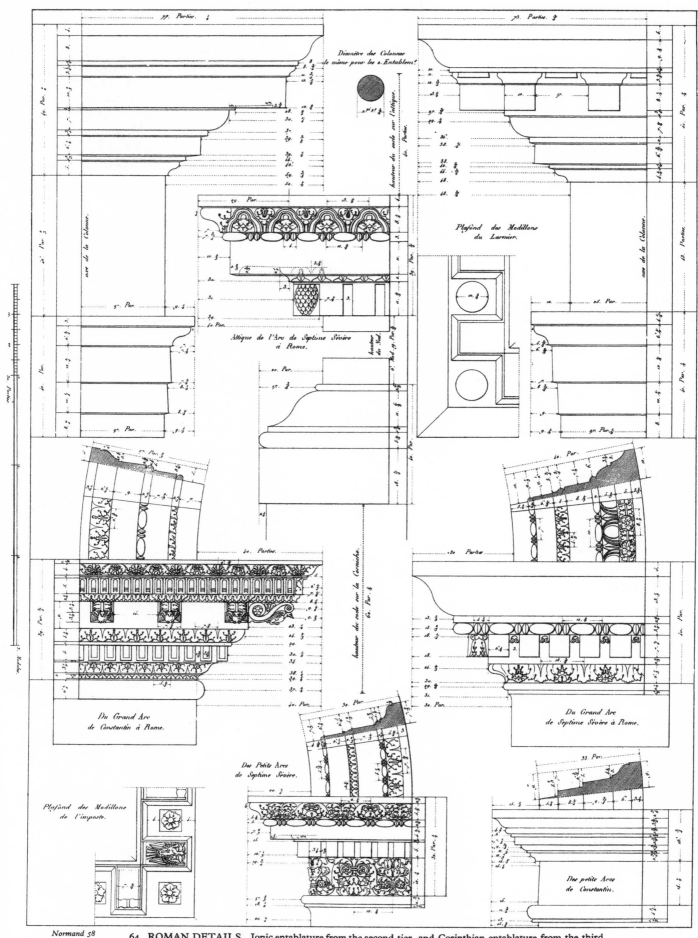

64. ROMAN DETAILS. Ionic entablature from the second tier, and Corinthian entablature from the third
tier of the Colosseum, Rome: Impost details from the arches of Septimius Severus and Constantine, Rome.

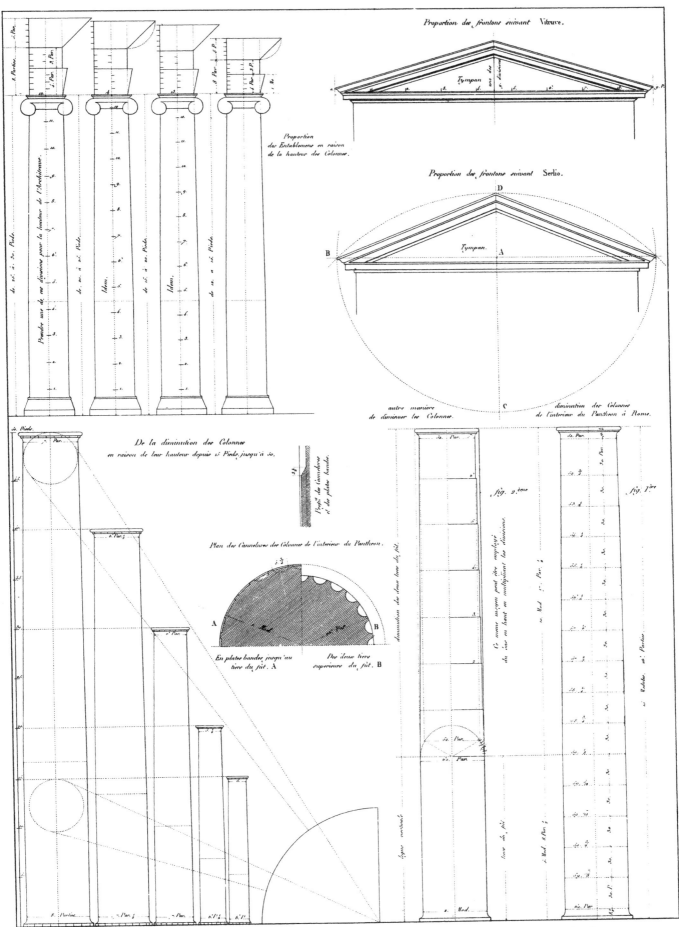

65. RULES for establishing proportions of entablatures and pediments, and the diminution and entasis of columns.

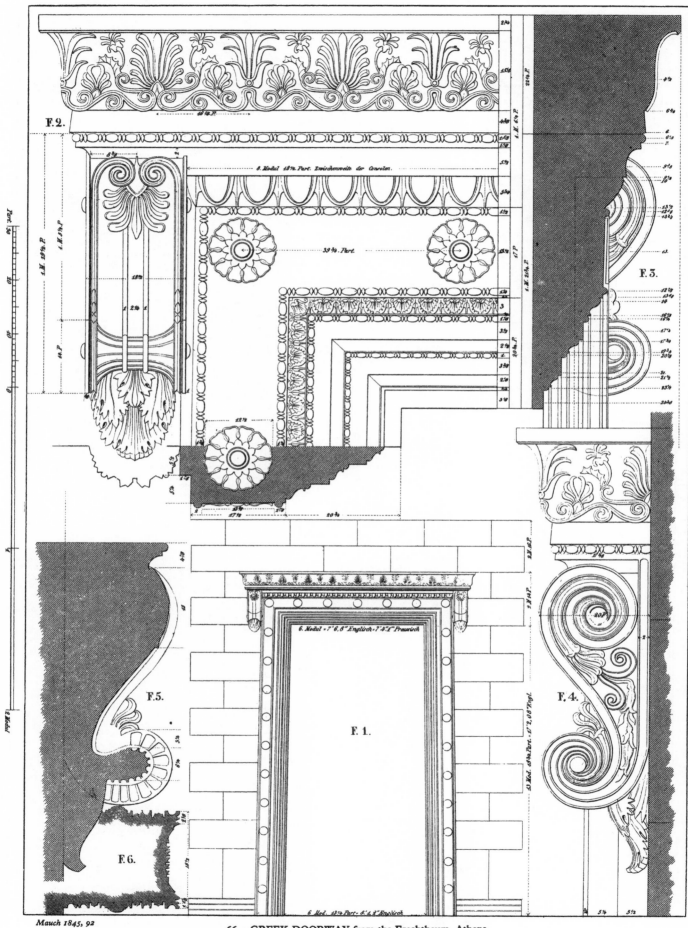

F.2.

F.3.

F.5.

F.6.

F.1.

F.4.

Mauch 1845, 92

66. GREEK DOORWAY from the Erechtheum, Athens.

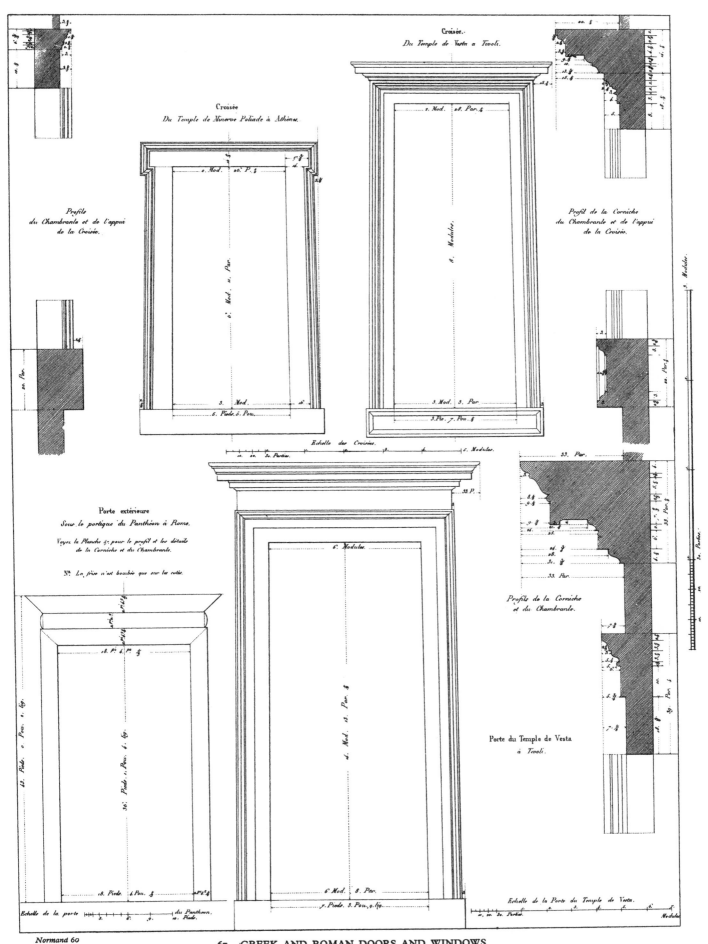

Croisée.
Du Temple de Vesta a Tivoli.

Croisée
Du Temple de Minerve Poliade à Athènes.

Profils
du Chambranle et de l'appui
de la Croisée.

Profil de la Corniche
du Chambranle et de l'appui
de la Croisée.

Echelle des Croisées.

Porte extérieure
Sous le portique du Panthéon à Rome.

Voyez la Planche 5. pour le profil et les détails
de la Corniche et du Chambranle.

N°. La frise n'est bombée que sur les cotés.

Profils de la Corniche
et du Chambranle.

Porte du Temple de Vesta
à Tivoli.

Echelle de la porte   du Panthéon.

Echelle de la Porte du Temple de Vesta.

Normand 60

67. GREEK AND ROMAN DOORS AND WINDOWS.

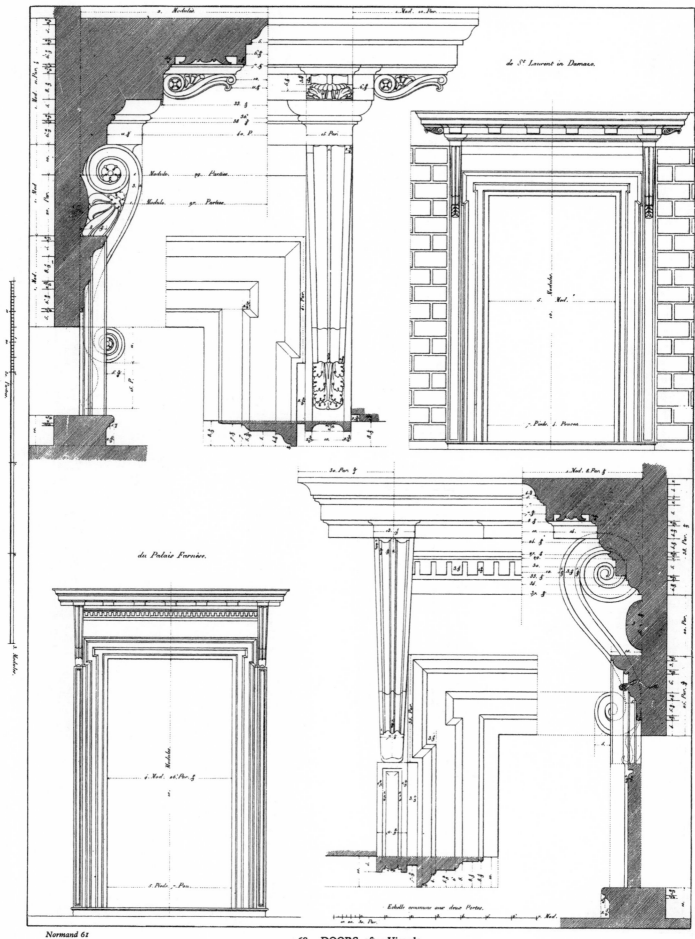

de St Laurent in Damaso.

du Palais Farnèse.

Echelle commune aux deux Portes.

68. DOORS, after Vignola.

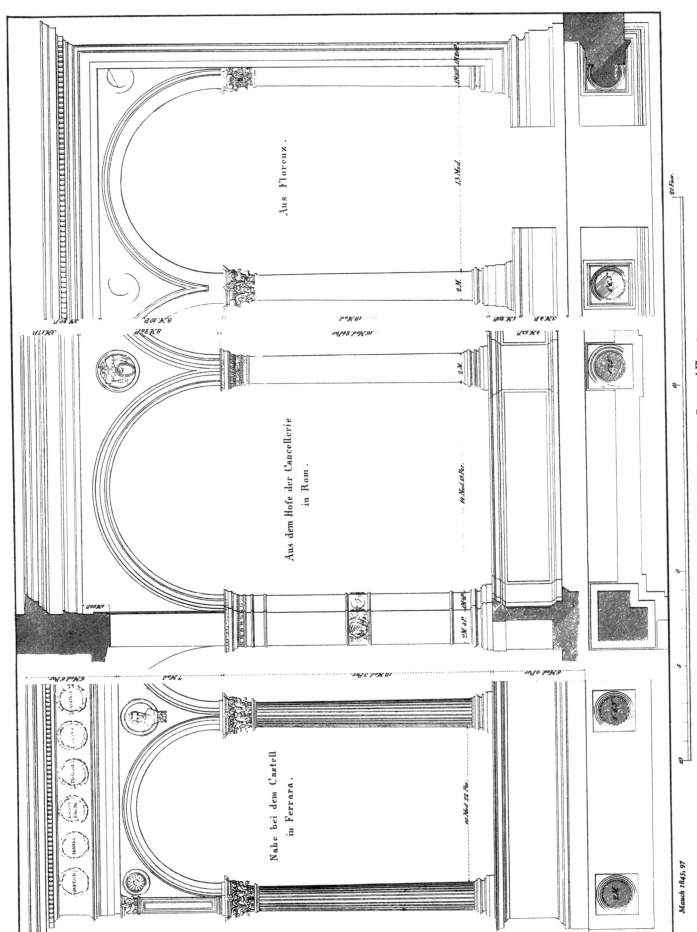

Aus Florenz.

Aus dem Hofe der Cancellerie
in Rom.

Nahe bei dem Castell
in Ferrara.

Mauch 1845, 97

69. RENAISSANCE ARCADES from Ferrara, Rome and Florence.

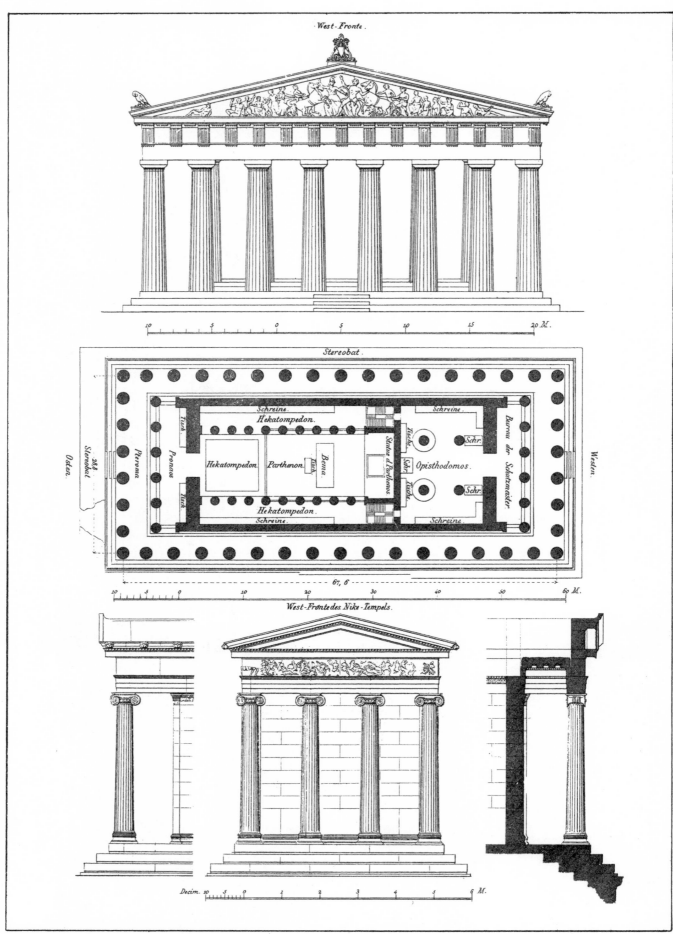

West-Fronte.

10   5   0   5   10   15   20 M.

Stereobat.

Schreine.
Hekatompedon.

Hekatompedon   Parthenon   Bema   Statue d. Parthenos   Opisthodomos.   Burau der Schatzmeister.

Schreine.
Hekatompedon.
Schreine.

Osten.   288 Stereobat.   Pteroma   Pronaos   Tisch   Tische   Schr.   Schr.   Westen.

67,6

10   5   0   10   20   30   40   50   60 M.

West-Fronte des Nike-Tempels.

Decim. 10   5   0   1   2   3   4   5   6 M.

Mauch 1875, 61

70. GREEK TEMPLE DESIGN. The Parthenon (*above*) and Temple of Niké Apteros, Athens.

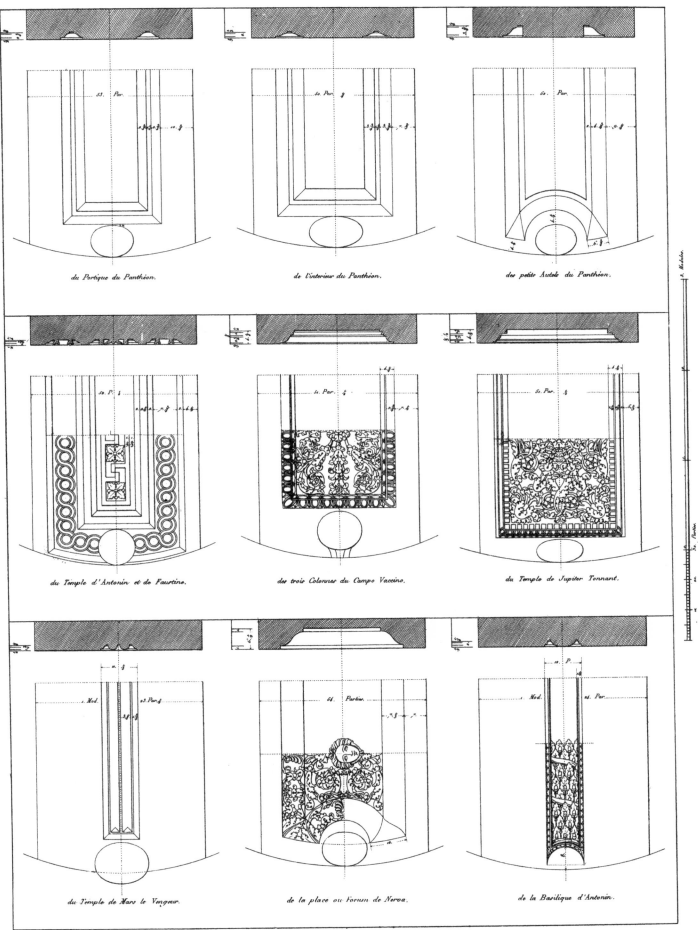

du Portique du Panthéon.

de l'interieur du Panthéon.

des petits Autels du Panthéon.

du Temple d'Antonin et de Faustine.

des trois Colonnes du Campo Vaccino.

du Temple de Jupiter Tonnant.

du Temple de Mars le Vengeur.

de la place ou Forum de Nerva.

de la Basilique d'Antonin.

Normand 62

71. SOFFITS of Roman architraves.

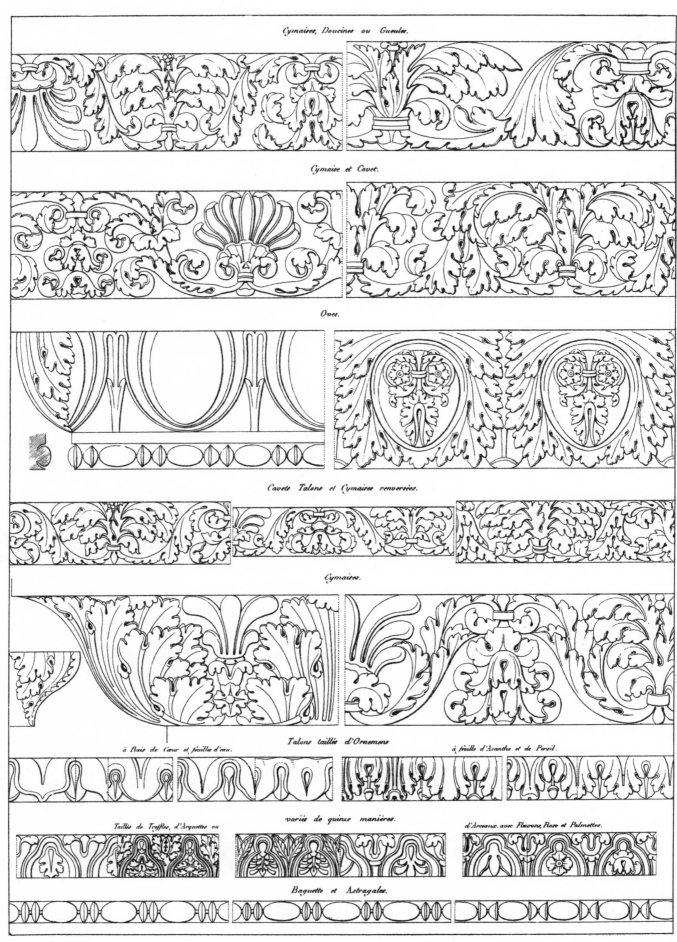

Cymaises, Doucines ou Gueules.

Cymaise et Cavet.

Oves.

Cavets Talons et Cymaises renversées.

Cymaises.

à Rais de Cœur et feuilles d'eau.   Talons taillés d'Ornemens   à feuille d'Acanthe et de Persil.

Taillés de Trefiles, d'Arguettes ou   variés de quinze manières.   d'Arceaux avec Fleurons, Rose et Palmettes.

Baguette et Astragales.